"*Everyday Miracles* is an insp......g text that articulates the intimate connection between the caring nature of God and the power of the human spirit. David Spangler has succeeded magnificently in describing the means through which every person can access abundance and experience a continual rapport with the energy that creates miracles. This book is delicious."
—Caroline Myss,
author of *The Creation of Health*

"In an age of infomercial messiahs and Internet apostles, what a joy it is to find a Christian mystic that is not on the make. David Spangler is the genuine article: a humble mystic in touch with infinity but never out of touch with humanity. Read him; the book will do you good."
—William Irwin Thompson, Ph.D.,
Founding Director,
The Lindisfarne Association

"Having recently experienced the beginnings of an inner shift away from nagging feelings of alienation and misanthropy toward a sense of the generosity of the present moment, I was delighted by *Everyday Miracles*. The warmth and clarity of David Spangler's wisdom is a wonder. As I read I feel as if he's taking my hand and leading me home to life."
—Richard Chamberlain,
actor

"David Spangler is one of the most profound and stimulating thinkers writing today, combining spiritual insight, metaphysical speculation, and scientific

discipline to explore the outermost reaches of the human condition."
—John Matthews,
author of *The Grail: Quest for the Eternal*

"A number of recent writers have set out to unveil our amazing power to manifest what we want; none have made it so clear that true effectiveness comes from choosing to align 'what we want' with the 'transpersonal will,' as Spangler terms it. His book is lively and easy to read; his clarity, simplicity, and deep wisdom are inspiring."
—Willis W. Harman,
President,
Institute of Noetic Sciences

DAVID SPANGLER

Everyday Miracles

The Inner Art of Manifestation

BANTAM BOOKS
New York Toronto London Sydney Auckland

EVERYDAY MIRACLES

A Bantam Book / January 1996

Library of Congress Cataloging-in-Publication Data

Spangler, David, 1945– .
   Everyday miracles : the inner art of manifestation / by David Spangler.
      p.   cm.
   ISBN 0-553-37542-3
   1. Spiritual life. 2. Occultism. 3. Miracles. 4. Spangler, David, 1945– .
   I. Title.
BL624.S657 1996
291.4′46—dc20   95-31725
                                                    CIP

Published simultaneously in the United States and Canada

PRINTED IN THE UNITED STATES OF AMERICA

FFG 10 9 8 7 6 5 4

To my mom and dad
Who introduced me to the Inner Art
And who manifested me in the first place

Contents

Acknowledgments

Many people have contributed to manifesting this book, and they all have my deepest gratitude and affection. Their help and support have made it possible for me to be a better writer and a better teacher than I otherwise would have been.

I want to thank in particular Toni Burbank and Jan Johnson, two of the finest editors any writer could ever hope to have. Their faith in and enthusiasm for this book, as well as their professional help, have been a source of real joy for me. Working with them has been a privilege.

Ned Leavitt, my agent, was also a wonderful source of support and help, in addition to getting this project off the ground in the first place. I am happy to count him a friend. Thanks, Ned!

On the home front, I literally could not have done this book without the help and advice of my wife, Julie, and the willingness of all my children to create an environment that enabled me to work. Thanks, John-Michael, Aidan, Kaitlin, and Maryn, for being quiet when I needed quiet and for playing with me when I got stuck! No one could ask for a better family. You are all my very best manifestation!

To John and Quita Cutrer and Hebron Cutrer, my partners in exploring manifestation, thank you for your support and insights. You also made this book possible.

I also want to thank William Irwin Thompson, a close friend who has encouraged me for years to write this book. Thanks for the title, Bill! And thank you to John and Caitlin, Bob and Josie, William and Sabrina, and Allen for comments and thoughts on the manuscript during its various stages of development. You have all been an inspiration for me. Also, thank you to Caroline Myss, whose insights into the healing process paralleled and enlarged my own insights into manifestation.

And finally, most important, thanks to all of you who participated with me both on-line and in person in the many classes and workshops on spirituality and manifestation that were the true genesis of this book. You were willing guinea pigs, testing all this material out and critiquing the various earlier forms of this book, for which I can never thank you all enough. Your stories of manifestation continue to inspire me!

Everyday Miracles

Introduction

What Is Manifestation?

What is manifestation? Let me begin with an example from my own life. For many years, I was a director of a nonprofit organization called the Lorian Association. Loosely organized, its associates were teachers and artists who lived and worked throughout the United States and Canada, keeping in touch through yearly gatherings, letters, and telephone calls. In 1980, a number of us decided to come together in Madison, Wisconsin, and develop a more centralized program. Two of our associates, Katherine and Roger Collis, rented a very large farmhouse outside the city, and we converted its lower floor into office space and classrooms, while the upper floor became living quarters. We also started a small publishing business. At first all went well; each of us who was teaching also traveled to do workshops and classes elsewhere, which brought in most of our personal income. However, as the work in Madison increased, it became obvious that we were going to need larger offices and a classroom, and that some of us would need to stop traveling and work for Lorian full-time. This meant having money for salaries. Even with the growth of our classes, we still did not have enough capital to make this move.

At this point, we decided to practice the inner art of manifestation. We drew up a budget based on what we felt we needed, and every week two or three of the other directors and I would meet early in the morning for breakfast and meditation together. We would use the budgets to visualize our needs, then we would attune to the new pattern of Lorian that we sought to manifest.

We had been doing this for a little over a month when out of the blue I got a long-distance phone call from a man who had read one of my books and wished to meet with me. I arranged a time for him to come to Madison. When he arrived, we talked for a couple of hours, then he came to the point. He was a successful businessman who was interested in spiritual issues; he felt blessed with abundance in his own life and wanted to share that blessing with others. Was there any way that he could help my work? I told him about Lorian and what we were seeking to do. Right on the spot, he offered a grant to Lorian that would cover our entire budget for two years. He also said that his oldest daughter was interested in the kind of spiritual and New Age subjects we were teaching; in addition to the grant, he would cover her expenses to move to Madison to take our new course, which would last for nine months, and he would pay her salary as well to work in our new office! Within two months, the money was in the bank, we had our new offices and classroom, and his daughter had joined us. We had performed a successful act of manifestation.

My Random House dictionary defines *manifestation* as the act of making something "readily perceived by the eye or the understanding; evident; obvious; apparent; plain." Manifestation is the act of making something invisible visible. It is the act of turning something abstract into something concrete and something potential into something real.

That's simple enough, and it's something we do in both conscious and unconscious ways every day. We make our thoughts plain and evident through our actions and our speech; in so doing, we are manifesting our ideas, our feelings, even our whole personalities. We do our work, and as a consequence, we manifest a product or a service.

Normally, we do this kind of manifesting in very ordinary ways in the physical world. We use familiar resources such as money, labor, or creativity to bring things we wish into our lives. But sometimes something we need or want just appears, as if by coincidence, without any seeming effort or unusual activity on our part. Or perhaps we learn to use resources of the mind and spirit that go beyond the ordinary world. Such resources get results—but not in the usual ways of buying or building.

This is what happened to us in Lorian. We did not take out a loan, seek a grant, or do any of the usual things a nonprofit organization does to raise capital. Outwardly we did nothing at all to achieve our goal. Inwardly, however, we were very active: creating, honing, and nourishing the image of what we wished to accomplish and what we needed in order to do it. We made that image a part of our lives and gave it the energy of our conviction and our love. In effect, we practiced the technique that I will be presenting to you in this book, and it worked beyond our expectations.

This kind of manifestation fulfills the Random House definition; something that was not obvious and evident before—the money we needed—became so. However, more is going on here than simply the act of making something "readily perceived by the eye or the understanding." We need a different, more expansive definition than that provided by the dictionary.

For our purposes in this book, I define manifestation as *the art of fashioning a co-creative, synchronistic, and mutually supportive relationship between the inner creative energies of a person's own mind and spirit and their counterpart within the larger world in order to bring a new and desirable situation into being.*

Manifestation often goes by other names. Sometimes it is called visualization, affirmation, or positive thinking, although I believe that these are only part of a larger process at work. Sometimes it is defined as a form of prayer or creative imagination. Whatever it is called, it is usually seen as a metaphysical, mystical, or magical process that can bring to us what we need or want when normal methods either have failed to do so or do not seem possible or applicable to the situation.

Manifestation seems to work in unpredictable, unanticipated, and maybe even miraculous ways. It could range from finding just the right parking place on a busy downtown street to being given a gift of money sufficient to pay your bills when you otherwise have no income; it could mean coincidentally finding just the right job or meeting just the right person with whom to fall in love. The flavor of a manifestation is that it seems coincidental, an event that happens synchronistically beyond the apparent power of our own efforts or resources yet that brings to us just what we need or want. It has the flavor of luck or magic about it. It appears miraculous.

One of my friends, David, relates the following experience: "While in college I decided to leave school and write a book about intentional communities and the people who were drawn to them. As both my writing experience and my finances were limited, I wasn't sure how I was going to pull this book off, but I felt very committed to the project. I decided to go on a ten-day yoga retreat to clear my thinking.

"The first night of the retreat was inwardly tormenting, as I experienced an inner dialog of 'Okay, now you've got ten days to figure this thing out' versus 'Just let go and let God have it. If it is meant to be, something will show up.' After a sleepless night, I was in morning meditation (with the battle still raging) when I made the decision to 'give it up' to spirit. This I did completely and fully, feeling like the proverbial 'ton of bricks' had been lifted from my soul!

"A few hours later, I was walking through a parking lot on my way to breakfast when a gentleman, leaning against a car, smiled and waved me over to him. He told me he was a writer and that he was attending the retreat to talk to people about their experiences in preparation for an article, and would I be willing to skip breakfast and talk to him. I agreed, and as we walked a short distance to a grove of trees, he asked a few questions about how I had come to the retreat and what I was experiencing. I told him of my interest in alternative communities and of my desire to write a book about them.

"By the time we reached the grove of trees, he said to me, 'Well, my wife and I are writers. We are renting a cottage with an extra bedroom and we have an extra typewriter—you can come stay with us for a while. I have published several books, written for some major magazines, and worked for NBC. I know the publishing circuit, so I can help out there. And don't worry about money, we'll work something out.' I was blown away! Here I had given my intentions up to spirit a few hours ago, and now I was getting my answer back on a silver platter! Talk about manifestation!"

In this book we will explore this inner art and how you may use it in your own life. I will share with you the philosophical, scientific, and spiritual principles and ideas I believe underlie and support manifestation. I will also lead you step-by-step through a personal manifestation project that illustrates each part of the process.

It is only fair to warn you at the outset that this inner art has two aspects. One is the level of acquisition. This is, I have found, what most people think of when they think of manifestation: the level of getting whatever it is that they desire. This is the practical, more mundane side.

The second level is the spiritual part of the art, and it makes certain demands on us. Manifestation is not really a tool like a hammer or a technique like special exercises to strengthen a particular muscle group in your body. It is not a "prosperity" technique. The forces that you will learn to work with in this book are forces woven into the fabric of your being—and into the beingness of everything else in the world as well. They are the deep creative energies that give all things form and existence. Therefore, on this level, manifestation is an art of incarnation. This level is also very practical, but in a deeper, more transformative way than simply learning how to acquire things.

When I teach manifestation, I affirm both levels. I teach the art of harmoniously shaping your world, but I also teach manifestation as a spiritual practice that aligns us with the deepest energies within creation.

In working with the principles of manifestation, we are asked to go beyond our surface images and probe in the dark, fertile areas that underlie our assumptions. We are asked to explore ourselves, our deeper thoughts and feelings so that we can begin to see just who we are manifesting and why. We are asked to encounter the same forces that act on seeds and bring them into the light from the nurturing hidden places or, on a cosmic scale, the forces that give birth to new worlds. In some ways these are ordinary, everyday forces, so common that we may overlook them; however, at the same time, they are forces of extraordinary power and mystery. These are not forces that hover around shopping malls and entice us with the latest consumer products. They are not forces of "prosperity," although they are forces of abundance.

Manifestation brings us into contact with a wilder, fiercer

energy than is represented by most techniques of affirmation, positive thinking, visualization, and the like. Often such techniques are based on a notion of "programming the unconscious." This metaphor may initially be useful, but it is wrong. The creative side of life is not a computer. It is more akin to the ancient woodland god Pan than to a Macintosh or an IBM. There is a wildness about it; it possesses a wet, flowing, green juiciness, a dancing sparkle of light, the power of lightning, the insistence of the plant that breaks through concrete in questing the sun. We do not "program" such forces. We honor them, we respect them, we work with them. They are companions, not slaves. Entering into manifestation is less an act of command than an act of communion and community. It is a participatory act, not an imperious one.

To understand the nature of this participation in a co-creative world is to understand the inner art of manifestation. The practice of such co-creation is the practice of this inner art. Underlying this understanding and practice is a simple principle. Manifestation is about *being*, not *getting*. If we honor this, we will not fail to manifest in skillful ways.

Chapter One

The Magical and the Ordinary

Which of the following stories is about manifestation?

A friend of mine works for the Washington state government. He has an office in Seattle and an office in Olympia, the state capital, and his job takes him all over the state seeking ways to promote the economic well-being of small businesses and the communities they serve. Every payday, he receives a check from the state, which he uses to support himself and his family.

As a self-employed lecturer and teacher, I have rarely known a regular payday. My income can fluctuate quite widely (and wildly) from one year to the next depending in part on the public interest in and response to my services. As the seventies drew to a close, there was a time when that interest waned. For two or three months, I found myself with plenty of time for study, reading, and pursuing various interests but without very much income. Beginning to feel desperate, I was starting to increase my efforts at manifestation when I received a letter from an organization I had never heard of before asking me to take part in a conference on the West Coast. The letter said that my expenses would be paid but mentioned nothing about fees (not an unusual situation in spiritual and New Age circles). When I read the letter, I had some doubt whether I should accept; I was living in Milwaukee at the time, and it was a long way to go. Further, the conference was being held at an inconvenient time for me. Then I had a strong intuition I should go in spite of the obstacles and even though I might not be paid anything. At the worst, I would have a nice trip to a part of the country I love very much, and at least I would have free meals for a few days! I went, had a wonderful time, and at the end of the conference was preparing to leave when one of the organizers came up and handed me an envelope. "Thank you, David," he said. "This is your share of the proceeds." Inside was a check for $16,000, which was almost a whole year's earnings for me in those days. A couple of months after that, I began a successful series of new classes and a number of lecture invitations arrived in the mail, so my financial needs were taken care of.

So which of these stories is an example of manifestation? Chances are you chose the second. Why?

Well, the first story about my friend seems so ordinary. What's special about earning a paycheck for doing one's job? Almost everyone does that or would like to. There's nothing unusual about it. For that matter, there may be nothing unusual about earning a large fee for lecturing; many public speakers do that. It was unusual for me, though. It was the largest amount I had ever been paid for a single event. What made it more special was the timing of it and the fact that if not for the intuitive flash that I had to go, I might well have turned the opportunity down. Furthermore, the invitation had literally come out of the blue from a group I had never even heard of.

Still, the outcome of the two stories is the same. Both my friend and I made money by doing a job. Was the money I earned more special because it came in an unexpected way rather than in a paycheck on a regular payday? Suppose I had not earned it through lecturing. From time to time over the years, I have received checks from people I don't know because they have read something I had written or heard a tape of a lecture I had given and had been helped by it. Usually these have been small gifts, less than a hundred dollars, most often less than fifty, but on a few occasions the amount has exceeded a thousand dollars. Whatever the sum, these gifts have always been deeply appreciated and they have almost always shown up just when I had a need. Is such money more magical or miraculous than what my friend or millions of people like him earn every month doing a job?

Let's explore this some more. Here are two more stories.

I love bread, all kinds of bread. Once when I was feeling in the mood for something special and different, I went down to a local bakery and discovered they had just baked Irish soda bread, one of my very favorites. There is something about the texture, the firm crust and the soft interior (like some people I've met), and the slightly sweet flavor that I truly enjoy. I love to heat up a slice, put a dollop of butter on it, and watch the butter spread like spring sunshine as it melts, and then smear it with a dark berry jam. Filled with this vision, my mouth already watering, I took out my wallet, handed the clerk some money, and bought a loaf to take home.

When I was ten years old, my mother and I accompanied my dad on a business trip around the Mediterranean. One of the stops we made was in Istanbul, Turkey. Late one evening, we went out from our hotel on a stroll through the city streets. Most of the shops were dark, but one bakery, though closed, was still lit up. Inside, the bakers were preparing their wares for the next day, and the smell of baking bread wafted out into the street. We stopped and watched the bakers at their work for a while, all the time wishing we had some of that fresh bread ourselves. Dad even tried knocking on the door, but a baker just smiled and waved us away. So we turned and walked away, our stomachs still rumbling at the thought of that bread.

We had gone only a couple of blocks when there was a loud whistle behind us. We stopped and turned. A policeman had appeared from nowhere and was running up the street toward us, waving to us to stop. Wondering just what was the matter—and feeling a little apprehensive, too—we waited until he caught up with us. He stopped, gave us a big smile and a salute, and then from behind his back he whipped out a large loaf of hot fresh bread! He had seen us looking in the bakery window and had had the bakers open up to sell him a loaf of bread to give to us, a gift of hospitality to the American tourists.

Which of those two stories is about manifestation?

The first story again seems so ordinary. I went down to a bakery and bought some bread. How nice, but so what? Anybody can do that. Millions of people in North America buy bread at the store every day. It's what keeps bakeries in business.

By contrast, the second story has magic in it. A need that we were unable to answer ourselves was met unexpectedly. We were given a gift. It was a romantic and chivalrous event, a sweet thoughtfulness extended by a representative of one culture to visitors from another who were guests in his land.

Still, was the bread we were given more special than the bread I bought? Was it different in some miraculous way? Was some magic woven into its very dough?

Speaking of miracles, here are two more stories.

I recently began to experience pain in my lower back. It is an occupational hazard for a writer, spending a lot of time as I do sitting. I did the usual things I do when this happens. I exercised. I went to my chiropractor. Nothing seemed to help, and the pain became worse, developing into sciatica. I then went to my naturopath for treatment, but after a couple of weeks in which the pain steadily increased and I found myself almost unable to walk, he sent me to an orthopedic surgeon. I was diagnosed as having a herniated disk in my lower back. As the doctor, a big man with a neatly trimmed beard and a slight European accent, talked with me, I began having visions of back surgery and weeks of convalescence. Then he said, "I do not think the condition is serious. It will probably heal itself in time, but what you must do is walk every day. You must walk your way through the pain, and the condition will clear up."

Just walk? No pills? No surgery? I couldn't believe it, but I felt a great relief. All I had to do was get out and move my legs. So I did. It was painful at first, but after a month of walking, the condition went away. My back had healed itself.

A friend of mine, Carol, once developed a pain in her back. As it got progressively worse, she went to have it examined and was told that one of the vertebrae in her back was disintegrating. She would need surgery to replace that disk, but the result would be that she would be unable to bend her back.

A few days before she was to go into surgery, she was lying in bed, unable to get up, talking to her husband. Suddenly they both heard what sounded like an explosion outside. Curious, her husband ran out to see what had happened, but he could find no evidence of anything amiss nor any indication of what might have caused the noise. When he came back, he discovered to his surprise Carol standing up and getting dressed, coming to see for herself whatever had happened. Distracted by the noise, she had felt a surge of energy and an impulse to get up and investigate. Filled with curiosity, it apparently didn't occur to her that she shouldn't be able to move at all! Later, she went to see her doctor, who took another X-ray. To his amazement, he discovered that the vertebrae were perfectly healthy. There was no sign of the disintegration that had been there previously. Her back was normal.

Which of these stories seems miraculous to you? Which seems ordinary?

I'm sure you probably picked the first story as ordinary, but why? Was the healing of my back less special, less magical, less meaningful than the healing of Carol's back? The stakes were not as high for me as they were for Carol, who faced a lifetime of reduced mobility. But whatever the stakes, in both instances, a physical condition was transformed and healing resulted.

What makes Carol's story—as well as the stories about the timely lecture invitation and the gift of the bread—magical is not the outcome but the process by which that outcome appeared. Especially in the medical cases, it was not a process that is familiar to us. We expect drugs to work, but when a healing occurs spontaneously or as a result of faith or some mental process, it carries a lot of mystery. There is wonderment involved, a sense of something happening that transcends the boundaries of the normal world most of us live in. In short, there is a feeling of the miraculous.

What differentiates manifestation from other forms of creation or acquisition, then, is not at the level of results. The outcome of our activities is the same whether we manifest or earn. The money in my pocket is worth the same and will buy the same things whether I receive it in a paycheck or find it mysteriously deposited on my doorstep by an unknown benefactor. I must still perform my tasks in a new job whether I was hired after interviews set up by an employment agency or whether I met my new employer in a lunch line and over a casual conversation was unexpectedly offered a job.

The difference between manifestation and acquiring things ordinarily often lies in the process. The former invokes deeper powers of the mind and spirit while the latter uses everyday methods such as buying, making, earning, and so forth. Yet even here the distinctions can blur. In the story I told above, I wasn't given $16,000. I earned it through the work I did at the conference. What I manifested was an opportunity.

Furthermore, nearly everything we have in our human world can be said to have emerged as a result of the powers of the mind and spirit. Imagination, creativity, insight, and the courage to explore and try new things are all intangible and ultimately mysterious and wondrous dimensions of the human psyche. Without them we would never have tamed fire, invented a wheel, built a city, planted a crop, baked bread, or painted a picture.

Opening to a Larger World

Yet for all the miracles and wonder implicit in everyday life, manifestation seems even more miraculous and wonderful. Partly this is because manifestation seems to represent getting something for nothing, something we would all like to do. Without apparently expending any effort, a situation that I need or want unfolds in my life. It's like getting a ticket to the fabled Diner of the Free Lunch.

By the end of this book, I hope you will realize that there is nothing free about manifestation, at least not in the sense of being just a one-way flow from the great breast of the universe into our hungry and ever-open mouths. It emerges from a relationship, and as such it does make demands upon us. It's not that we don't do anything in order to manifest. It's that we do different things and tap resources within ourselves different from what we may be used to doing.

More than being a handout from some great cosmic welfare state, manifestation is a gift. Unlike a handout, which can be impersonal and ultimately disempowering and demeaning, a gift comes with a sense of caring and affirmation. A mindful gift comes with love. It is an act of community, even of communion.

Manifestation suggests that the universe really is a friendly place and that we are part of a community that cares about our well-being. When we hear a story of manifestation, beyond the surface details lies this deeper implication: There is a spirit of caring in the universe that will meet our needs if we give it the opportunity. In a culture like ours, whose sinews have been strengthened by competition and whose soul has been forged in a masculine flame of struggle and conquest, this really is a magical and wondrous notion.

Manifestation also suggests that there are principles at work in the world for which a purely materialistic philosophy cannot account. There is a medieval woodcut that shows the earthly world contained within a great bubble. Outside the bubble lies a celestial realm filled with stars and moons and with the mechanisms that make creation run. In the picture, a man is poking his head through the bubble and gaining a glimpse of that wondrous creative realm that had previously been invisible to him. When we experience an act of manifestation or hear about one that happened to someone else, it is as if our head has momentarily burst through that bubble, and the intimations of a new world lie spread out before us.

As I have traveled and lectured over the years, I have consistently found in audiences and people I have worked with a hunger for this magic, this sense that all around us is an expanded world of wonder, power, and caring. It is easy to be cynical about this desire; few of us may wish to admit to having it because it can leave us so painfully vulnerable. To open ourselves to the possibilities of that larger world is to reclaim an innocence that can easily be mistaken for naïveté or childishness. Yet the hunger is there and cannot be denied. It can drive us to find adventure, thrills, drama, and escape in the material world, or it can empower us to look inward, to find within ourselves a gateway into that larger world. In either case, it causes us to search for a missing vitality in our lives.

It is this sense of new vitality, of awakening to being alive in a large and wondrous place, that lies at the heart of the practice of manifestation. The magic of this inner art is neither in the outcome nor in the process but in ourselves and our relationship to life. In this sense, it is truly an art and not just a technique. The art of a poet lies not only in her words; the art of a painter lies not only in his choice of colors; it lies in the ability of each to engage vitally with life in a way that draws a quality of soul out of each. Then an expansion of feeling and perception, of life and energy, takes place that transcends the form of the craft. Likewise, manifestation lies not just in the acquisition or creation of something but in the crafting of a fuller relationship with life.

Like art, manifestation makes soul visible. It demonstrates not just that manifestation can be miraculous but that *we* are miraculous and that *life* is miraculous. We may live in the midst of the ordinary, but that ordinariness emerges from and rests upon a foundation of the extraordinary.

In our lives we recognize times and events that are miraculous and magical and times that are dull and "ordinary." However, this recognition says less about the situation itself or the things themselves than about our own state of perception. It is as much our relationship to the thing or the situation that makes it magical as any quality inherent in the thing or situation itself. Seen in the proper context, receiving a paycheck after doing honest and well-performed labor can be just as magical as having a check arrive out of the blue from some unknown friend. The difference between the miraculous and the ordinary exists in our minds, not in reality.

This is an important insight, because the power that lies

behind manifestation arises from a state of wholeness. Life itself does not make such distinctions as "ordinary," "extraordinary," "miraculous," or "magical." Everything just is, and its *isness* is sufficient. The universe is seamless, yet we often divide it up into separated segments, cutting ourselves off from the power of the whole. We speak of the division between spirit and matter, between soul and personality, between the magic of manifestation and the labor of ordinary work. Yet spirit and matter, soul and personality, magic and labor, the extraordinary and the ordinary are all aspects of one reality, one flow of energy and events. It is the vision and experience of this wholeness that we wish to cultivate, for it is the source of power for our acts of manifestation.

Dividing our lives into "magical" and "ordinary" categories reduces or interferes with our creative energy. Any artist knows this. To say that some things are worth looking at because they are special and others are not is to reduce our lives to an endless quest for scenic lookout points, missing the scenery that is actually all around us. The end result is a kind of creeping blindness in which we eventually fail to see the magic even in the magical.

A friend of mine accuses me of always wanting to demystify the extraordinary. He accuses me of looking for God in a peanut butter sandwich. To this I plead guilty (after all, what could be more divine than peanut butter, which I love!), but my motive is not to strip life of miracles and wonder, giving everything a bland sameness. It is just the opposite. I want to make the ordinary miraculous and the miraculous ordinary. Otherwise, I feel we make the everyday, familiar aspects of our lives too ordinary, denying them the magic and miracles that actually are there, while making the extraordinary aspects of our lives too special and magical, making them accessible only under special conditions (or even worse, assuming that only special people with unique inner talents can enjoy such moments and that manifestation is a technique just for the few). The ordinary becomes too drab, and the extraordinary too different, requiring some unique moment or effort to attain it. Our energy becomes split between enduring the ordinary and aspiring toward the special. In either event, we lose the unique creativity that is found only in full attentiveness to the present moment, whatever its form. It is out of that attentiveness that magic blooms.

Learning the inner art of manifestation is a paradoxical process. Unless we can see the magic in the ordinary routines and things of everyday life—or perhaps I should say, unless we can see those ordinary things in a fresh, mindful, and magical way—we will not be able to fully invoke the inner power that fuels the everyday miracles of manifestation.

I began this chapter by comparing stories. Which of them are stories of manifestation? They all are, of course. They represent different techniques at work, and in some of the stories the technique or the processes take us into layers of reality—and mystery—that draw on nonordinary capabilities of the human soul and psyche. But all the stories represent the magic of manifestation at work. When you understand that and can find the magical and miraculous in the ordinary and mundane, then you will truly be on the path to mastering the inner art of manifestation.

Chapter Two

Learning to Manifest: My Personal Story

My introduction to the art of manifestation was one that most people probably have received in one form or another. That was instruction in the power of prayer. As a child, I was taught to turn to God when I had a need that seemingly could not be met by any ordinary means, to state my needs in prayer, and then to have faith that those needs would be met. Prayer and faith were vital parts of our family life.

The Power of Mind

In 1952, Methodist minister Dr. Norman Vincent Peale published a book, *The Power of Positive Thinking*, that became a great best-seller. In it he detailed the power that mental attitudes and imagery have to affect one's life. He later wrote other books along the same line, including *Positive Imaging: The Powerful Way to Change Your Life*, published in 1982.

My parents were married by Dr. Peale in 1939 and always held him in high regard. Consequently, his books occupied a special place on our family bookshelves. As taught by Dr. Peale, the idea that our thoughts, feelings, and attitudes influence what we attract into our lives became integral to our family beliefs.

When I was a teenager, my parents and I attended a Unity church for a period of time. The Unity Church of Christianity, a religious movement like Christian Science, Ernest Holmes's Science of Mind, and Religious Science, grew out of a stream of teaching and philosophy that in its American incarnation had begun in the early part of the nineteenth century with the Transcendentalist movement of Emerson and Thoreau. In particular, Unity grew from the teachings of Phinias P. Quimby, a New England clockmaker, who formulated a system of mental imagery and positive thinking that he claimed would create beneficial changes in a person's life. This system became known as New Thought. It held that consciousness or mind is the primary creative force in the cosmos, all things having ultimately derived from the "Universal Mind" of God.

This idea did not originate with the Transcendentalists or with Quimby, however. Many modern techniques and ideas of positive thinking, visualization, and manifestation come from the mystery traditions of East and West, so called because they sought to explore the mysterious, invisible, creative forces underlying the world of form using psychological and spiritual means. Alchemy, Rosicrucianism, and what historian Frances Yates calls the "Hermetic-Cabalist" tradition were among those that taught the controlled and disciplined use of the will and imagination to create changes in consciousness, which in turn would initiate changes in one's life and environment.

So as a child and as a teenager, I was raised with the idea that we help shape our own reality through our thoughts and feelings. Though I don't remember the word *manifestation* ever being used by either of my parents, I learned from an early age some key elements of belief and practice that make manifestation possible.

The Road to Findhorn

In 1964 when I was in college pursuing a degree in biochemistry and molecular biology, a friend of mine sponsored a large conference on spirituality and psychic phenomena. Knowing that I had some experience in these areas, my friend invited me to be one of the speakers. It was the first time I had spoken publicly about my contact and interactions with spiritual worlds, a connection that I had developed since I had had a series of mystical and psychic experiences as a young child. This talk led to a number of invitations to travel and speak to other groups, but at the time I did not feel it was right to respond, since my college studies kept me very busy. The following year, however, I had a strong intuition that I should follow through on some of these invitations. So in the summer of that year I went to Los Angeles to work with a group there and later moved up to the San Francisco area. I fully intended to return to college and finish my degree work, but as it turned out, I never did. One invitation led to another, and I soon discovered I was fashioning a career for myself as a lecturer and facilitator in areas of spiritual development and human relations. I laughingly called myself a "free-lance mystic," something that I still am today.

I often didn't know at the beginning of the month where the money would come from to pay the rent and the bills by the end of the month. Yet I never had any doubt that my needs would be met, and they always were. I was following the call of my inner spirit, and as long as I paid attention to my intuition, I knew I would be all right.

Mostly, I lived on what I was paid for classes I designed and taught. There were often times, though, when money or other resources would be given to me in unexpected ways just at the moment when I needed them, enabling me to continue or broaden my work. I rarely used the word *manifestation* in my work, yet manifesting was exactly what I was doing.

However, I was learning to manifest in different ways than I had learned while at home. Increasingly, I was not using the traditional methods of visualization, affirmation, or positive thinking, at least not as my primary technique. Instead, I was learning to go inward in my consciousness to a place where I could sense the soul or essence of what I needed or of the situation I wished to create. I was learning to attune to that essence and to bring it into my own inner being, aligning it with my own creative presence and incorporating its "flavor" or presence into my daily life. Most of the time, in fact, I did not focus on a specific need. I simply affirmed that there was a presence within me that knew all my needs, even those I hadn't yet realized, and that this presence was in touch with a creative power that could meet those needs fully and lovingly.

One time I wanted to write and produce some booklets for my students to use. At the time, all I had was an old portable typewriter that I had used in college. It was sufficient for most of my everyday work but not for producing manuscripts good enough for printing. Nor did I have the money to pay for a big printing job. While I was pondering just how to deal with this problem, I received a phone call from the husband of one of my students. He said that he appreciated how I had helped his wife, and he wanted to do something for me. Since he owned an office supply shop, how would I feel if he outfitted an office for me, including a new typewriter, a new mimeograph machine, a desk, a chair, and anything else I needed?

So within a week I found myself in a new rent-free office with all the up-to-date equipment I needed to write and produce the booklets I needed for my classes. I ended up using this office for over a year until I began traveling and no longer had need of it. I am still grateful to this man for his kindness at a time when it meant a great deal to me and my work.

As I traveled and lectured around the United States and Canada from 1966 to 1969, I occasionally ran into someone who had been to a small community near the ancient fishing village of Findhorn in the north of Scotland. There, I was told, the people were talking with nature spirits and using their advice and help to grow a miraculous garden. It was the kind of story that one often encounters when working in the metaphysical world, and I pictured a group of eccentric but kindly British psychics puttering away in their gardens and chatting with little fairies and elves.

I frankly didn't think too much about the Findhorn community. However, in 1970, I traveled to Britain to do some work and decided to take a few days to visit this place I had heard so much about. By then I had also read about it and knew more of its story.

Findhorn is on a peninsula that juts out into the Moray Firth, a large bay leading in from the North Sea. As it happens, the warm currents of the Gulf Stream that flow up and around the north of Scotland create an unusual climate around Findhorn. It has more clear, sunny days than any other place in Britain with the exception of some of the southern beaches. Consequently, vacationers from Glasgow and Edinburgh would come up to Findhorn in the summer to bask in the warm sun on the beach, and many of them stayed in holiday trailers and tents at the Findhorn Bay Caravan Park, which was almost on the beach itself.

In 1962 an ex-RAF officer named Peter Caddy, his wife, Eileen, their three sons, and a friend and colleague, Dorothy Maclean, arrived at the park. Peter, Eileen, and Dorothy were temporarily out of work. Lacking other accommodation and to save money, they had decided to live in the Caddy trailer, onto which they would build a small annex for Dorothy. Peter, though, was a highly trained executive who had run a large three-star hotel, and Dorothy was an executive secretary; they did not expect to remain unemployed for long. However, as one job opportunity after another fell through, some in very mysterious ways, they realized that their stay on this trailer park might be longer than they had anticipated.

For many folks, this might have been a disheartening realization. Peter, Eileen, and Dorothy, however, had worked together for years, and each followed a spiritual discipline of meditation and tuning in to inner guidance. In their meditations, they were told that in fact they had been planted in this trailer park to do a spiritual work, and that the first step they should take was to grow a garden.

There was plenty of available space around them to do this, but the soil was little more than sand and gravel, and the wind blowing in from the North Sea was salty and harsh. It was not the best situation for growing a garden. It was at this juncture that Dorothy received a message one morning in her daily meditation. This message said that behind all the phenomena of nature were intelligent spiritual beings, like angels, and that she should contact them for help. She did this, and to her amazement, she found herself in contact with these beings, whom she called *devas*, a Sanskrit word meaning "shining one."

Over the next few years, Dorothy received hundreds of messages from these devas, many of them giving very practical detailed instructions on how to grow their garden, instructions that she and Peter would carefully follow out. With both physical and spiritual nourishment, the garden flourished and became a phenomenon, eventually attracting worldwide attention. Others came to join them and share their work and contact with the world of spirit. Then, in 1970, a wave of people descended on them. By the late seventies, the community had grown to more than three hundred people.

I arrived in the late summer of 1970 as part of that first wave, most of whom, like me, were from the United States. When I got out of the car that had brought me from the local train station, I was astonished at what I found. The lush and beautiful gardens and the people I saw seemed to sparkle with light and life. There was a spirit and a magic about the place that was positively invigorating and uplifting. I knew immediately that this was a place where I wanted to spend some time.

As it turned out, the founders of the community had the same intention for me. I had no sooner arrived than Peter Caddy came out of his bungalow and immediately gave me a bear hug. "Welcome, David!" he exclaimed. "It's so good to have you here. We've been expecting you for three years!" Seeing my bewilderment at this remark, he laughed and said, "Come on in for tea and meet my wife, Eileen. We have a story to tell you."

Three years earlier, a friend of mine had sent to Peter and Eileen one of the booklets I had written and mimeographed for my classes (using, as I related above, the equipment that had been given to me). When Eileen read the booklet, she had had an inner vision that I would one day come to Findhorn and play an important role in the community's growth and work. Now that vision had finally come true. Within two days of my arrival, I had become a co-director of the community along with Peter and Eileen.

Findhorn became my home for the next three years. It was an exciting place to be and an exciting time to be there as the community began to grow and take shape. It was also the place where my insights into manifestation truly took shape and where I began to formulate the ideas and techniques that I will be sharing with you.

The "Laws" of Manifestation

If ever a place were built with manifestation, Findhorn was it. The teaching and practice of manifestation were a core part of the community's belief system and development.

Manifestation took two related forms in the community. On the one hand, Eileen Caddy's method was simply to have faith and trust in God. "All your needs will be perfectly met if you have faith," her guidance told her. And she, Peter, and Dorothy definitely had abundant faith born from years of spiritual training.

On the other hand, Peter had also been taught the power of visualization, affirmation, and positive thinking—which he called the laws of manifestation. He gave a talk every day on these laws and principles to the many visitors that came to the community. He was filled with stories about how the community had met its needs through positive thinking and visualization. His enthusiasm, confidence, conviction, and charm as a storyteller made these techniques of manifestation come excitingly alive for everyone who heard him.

These techniques are probably familiar to anyone who has any interest in manifestation. They are taught in popular books such as *Psycho-Cybernetics* by Maxwell Maltz and *Creative Visualization* by Shakti Gawain, as well as in the writings of Dr. Peale, Napoleon Hill, the Reverend Robert Schuller, and hundreds of others.

They are easy to describe. *Visualization* requires forming a mental picture as fully as you can of what you wish to manifest. You must see it and experience it clearly in your mind's eye. In forming this image, you should use as many of your senses as possible, imagining not only what the objective looks like but, where appropriate, what it sounds like, smells like, tastes like, and feels like. It must become real to you in your imagination. To help this process, you might use props such as pictures of the object of your manifestation, if such are available, or you could draw a picture or use some symbol that suggests this image to you and reinforces its reality.

Once you have an image clearly in mind, you create a positive, reinforcing statement about it. This is an *affirmation*. It should be a real-time statement about what is happening now, not what might or will happen in the future. So if you want to manifest a new car, your affirmation might be, "I am now the proud owner of a new Honda Civic." You then repeat your affirmation at different times of the day in order to reinforce the reality of what you are manifesting. There is no doubt that repetition can serve to make an image more real for us, and it is the reality of the image that carries the power to make it come true.

Positive thinking is a general attitude that does not allow doubt or questioning to interfere with your affirmation and visualization. You do not repeat your affirmation and then add "I hope" or "maybe." You do not cast doubts on your process by thinking that this manifestation isn't really going to work. You do not undermine your efforts with negative, self-defeating, self-questioning attitudes.

These techniques have many advantages. They are simple, straightforward, and easily learned. They help develop the imagination and cultivate a positive attitude toward life. And most important, they work.

They certainly worked at Findhorn, and not just for Peter, Eileen, and Dorothy. People manifested trailers to live in, tools to work with, and money for projects. Once I happened to stop by the trailer of a young man who lived in the community. I noticed that he had pictures of guitars all over one wall. Noticing my interest, he said, "I'm manifesting a guitar. I have these pictures up to help me visualize it and to remind me of my affirmations." Sure enough, within a couple of months, he had his guitar, a surprise gift from one of the visitors to the community.

As I settled into my new role as co-director, I joined Peter in his daily meetings with visitors, listening to him tell the story of how the community had developed, and in particular the role that the laws of manifestation had played in that development. Peter, tall, wide-shouldered, ruddy-faced, wearing a bulky pull-over, and looking like the RAF officer or the successful manager of a hotel that he had been, would beam like one of the nearby coastal lighthouses and tell the stories of how everything in the community had been manifested. Every day he would tell the same stories with a zest and gleefulness matched only by his own ever-present vitality. He was like a fisherman telling how he had reeled in the big one or a quarterback describing the crucial play that won the championship, his voice crackling with delight. And people would go away inspired, convinced that whatever they wanted in their lives was only an affirmation away if they could just be as positive as Peter.

Every day I would marvel at how he made the stories seem fresh and new, as if he were telling them for the first time, and for the first few weeks, caught up in Peter's infectious enthusiasm, I always felt as if I were hearing them for the first time. However, in time I began to reflect upon my own experiences with manifestation. I realized that whatever it was I had been doing over the years to manifest, it wasn't by using the laws of manifestation in the way Peter was describing.

To begin with, while I certainly had a positive outlook on life, I did not practice positive thinking in the sense of always casting out any feelings of doubt, fear, or uncertainty as soon as they entered my mind. For Peter, doubt did not exist. For me, doubt was not necessarily a disempowering emotion but a message, another bit of information about the situation at hand. While I did not want to be ruled by doubt or fear, I did not want to ignore them either. Something about always concentrating on the light, bright, positive side of life seemed out of balance to me. It denied my ability to recognize and confront the shadow side of existence. If I were having doubts or fears, then I wanted to examine them, not cast them aside. Otherwise, it seemed to me, I ran the risk of denying some aspect of reality or suppressing honest questioning or critical judgment.

Likewise, I never used affirmations. Affirmations are often presented by teachers of manifestation techniques as a way of "programming" the unconscious as we would program a computer. I have never liked this metaphor of the mind as a kind of biological computer. It seems to me to oversimplify the biological and psychospiritual characteristics of the brain/mind phenomenon.

However, this metaphor is apt in another sense, for a program in a real computer not only directs the work of the machine in a particular and powerful way, it also limits it. If I program a computer to write, it is not going to draw pictures, although a picture might be a better mode of communication for what I want to say. By mindlessly and repetitively affirming a particular kind of manifestation, I might miss opportunities to manifest in a different way. My affirmations can become a substitute for the passion and mindful intentionality that is so much a part of creativity.

Visualization, too, has always been problematical for me. Being partly deaf (and having no sense of smell at all), I have always been visually oriented. However, when I turn inward with my inner sight, I don't usually see things as shapes but as patterns or as radiances that suggest the essence or spirit of what I am perceiving. Also, in trying to create a clear, precise image to visualize, I may actually narrow my options. If I know exactly what I want, then this is not a problem. However, often I may have a need and I think I know just what will meet it, but in fact there is something better out there that I don't know about. By being too specific, I may reduce the chance that that better manifestation will take place because I am focusing my energy upon that with which I am familiar. Or it may take place and I don't recognize it because it came in a form I wasn't expecting. I may limit myself to what I can imagine and visualize based on what I already know.

In short, I found the techniques of visualization, affirmation, and positive thinking to be useful and powerful in some situations. But I found they imposed limitations upon my creativity, imagination, and my powers of manifestation. They certainly could focus the power of the mind, but as I listened to Peter, I began to realize that there was more to manifestation than just those powers. There was a deeper force at work as well, and it was attunement to that force that constituted the core of my approach to this inner art, an approach that up to that time I had never attempted to fully articulate or explain.

I was not the only one challenged by the idea of manifestation. Over time it became a challenge for many in the community as well. As more and more people joined the community and the number of visitors grew into the hundreds, it became physically impossible for Peter to continue meeting with everyone and sharing the Findhorn stories as intimately as he had done in the past. It was one thing to walk through the community with Peter in a small group of about a dozen, examining the pottery studio, the weaving looms, the print shop with its offset printer, the dining room, the greenhouse, and all the other buildings and tools and to hear firsthand from Peter the stories of their manifestation. It was quite another to sit in a group of a hundred or more and hear the same stories, often from a community member who had been delegated to be the host for the day. Something vibrant in Peter's presence—vitality, innocence, conviction, the security of a man who has stepped off into the abyss of faith and has found himself supported—transformed the stories from mere recitals of acquisition. They became jewels in a crown of trust and abundance that any person could wear.

In the lives of Peter, Eileen, and Dorothy, the point was not the manifestation of worldly goods; the point was surrender to God. Underneath the stories ran a current of joy that we all live in a universe that loves us, embraces us, and wishes only for our highest good. That universe was a reality to the founders of Findhorn because they had won their way into it through twenty years of hardship, discipline, struggle, pain, and faith. When you talked with them or listened to them or simply were in their presence, you knew they weren't manifesting things; they were manifesting the presence of God's love. They had learned to put God first above any personal considerations; having done so, they found their needs being met in wondrous ways. It was that perspective that was at the core of the stories.

However, when the same stories were told by others, they became simply myths of acquisition. They were exciting, yes, and wonderful, and filled with promise, but still they tended to lose their connection to a higher level of meaning and became superficial stories of magical events and extraordinary happenings.

The consequence was that the laws of manifestation took on magical overtones. Rather than being a living art that one can play with, they became like sacred rules that one had to obey lest evil descend, or like incantations and rituals that, if followed exactly, would bring riches.

People began to come to me to ask why their manifestations weren't working. In almost every case, they had done everything just the way they had heard that Peter, Eileen, and Dorothy had done—visualizing, affirming, keeping positive—but nothing was happening. As they recounted their efforts, I realized that they were basically performing a technique by rote. They were engaged in a mental process disconnected from any deeper levels of attunement, passion, or soul. They were people doing a ritual whose meaning and purpose had been forgotten: The form was there but the spirit was not.

Like any art, there must be room in the process of manifestation for spontaneity, for the unexpected and the inspired. When it is treated as a magical technique rather than as an art, however, manifestation can become inflexible. It becomes a competition between the manifestor and the universe, a contest of wills rather than the sharing and mutual giving of two lovers.

One week at Findhorn our task list included laying floor tiles in a room we were converting into a classroom. No one in the community had the particular expertise this task required. The night before we needed to begin, a middle-aged man carrying a backpack walked into the community and was given a place to stay. When he introduced himself the next morning at the daily community meeting where everyone received their job assignments, he said he was on a walking tour of Scotland. He had heard good things about the community and wanted to stay for a few days. When asked what his job was, he said he was a professional tile layer!

Peter immediately whisked him up to the classroom and showed him the floor and the tiles that were to be laid. "This is your job while you are in the community. We needed a professional tile layer, and you showed up right on schedule. You were manifested, you know!" Standing nearby, I could already see the next chapter in Findhorn's saga of manifestation being written in Peter's mind.

However, like a character in a novel who rebels at an author's intent, the man looked at Peter, looked at the tiles, and replied, "I can appreciate you need a tile layer, but that's not what I'm going to do in the community. I do that every day for a living. I want to do something different for my vacation."

"But you don't understand," Peter replied. "You see, this is how the laws of manifestation work. We had a need for a tile layer, we visualized a tile layer coming to the community, and you showed up on the very day we needed you. You are our manifestation!"

"No, I'm not," he insisted, "and if you keep pressuring me about this, I shall leave! I am here to do something else."

"Well, you can do what you want in the community after you lay the tiles, but the tiles need to be laid, we need someone with professional knowledge and experience to lay them, and you have showed up on the very day. It's obvious. You are the one we manifested to do this job."

"In that case, you have just demanifested me!" With that the man turned around and left, and we never saw him again. Later Peter and I had a good laugh about this, but it was one manifestation story that unfortunately never made it into the official canon of the history of Findhorn.

Perhaps most ominously, as the community grew and its needs expanded proportionately, I began to notice that a kind of subtle pressure was developing to insure that everyone was thinking positively. Negative thoughts were seen as obstructions that might cut off the flow of resources into the community. Any feelings or thoughts that were not "positive" or uplifting were potentially dangerous to the community because they would block manifestation. Sometimes in community meetings, individuals who questioned or doubted a particular course of action were accused outright of bringing in negative energies that would sabotage what Findhorn was trying to do; there were even suggestions that if such people couldn't "get out of their personalities" and be positive in their thinking, then they should leave.

Of course, in any community, this approach is a dangerous step toward developing a coercion to obey a party line and engage in conformist thinking. It ultimately diminishes freedom and creativity within the group. Left unchecked, it could have destroyed the community. At the very least, this attitude meant that a lot of distressful feelings and thoughts became suppressed under a superficial layer of positive thinking. The dark side of the community was denied in order that the light side might be emphasized and given more power. People felt stymied in expressing their darker feelings, and this ironically began to impact negatively on the community's ability to do its work properly as well as to manifest.

The ramifications of the situation were not lost on Peter. He wanted a certain positive tone to be set by the community that would be inspirational and empowering to the hundreds of visitors. But he did not want conformity. On the other hand, he did not want people spreading a lot of doubt and fear in the community that would undermine its powers of manifestation. He could recognize that in some ways the idea of the laws of manifestation, so clear and workable to him, was becoming unclear and misunderstood in the community at large.

By this time, I had shared with Peter my own feelings that there was more to manifestation than the kind of positive thinking, visualization, and affirmation techniques that he was teaching. He agreed and then challenged me to present a series of lectures to the community that would explore that deeper range. "We'll call them lectures on the *new* laws of manifestation!" he exclaimed.

So a time came when I had to pull together all my scattered thoughts, intuitions, experiences, and concerns about manifestation and finally articulate just what manifestation meant to me as an inner art that was more than just a magical or mental technique.

It wasn't easy for me to do, and at the time, over twenty years ago, there was much that I wasn't able to put into words. Still, I did the best I could, and the resulting lectures seemed to have the desired effect of lessening the pressure that had built up around a superficial understanding of manifestation.

After I left Findhorn in 1973 and returned to the United States, these lectures were gathered together and published as a small book called *The Laws of Manifestation*. This book proved very popular and enjoyed wide sales for a number of years. However, I was never fully satisfied with this material, as I felt there were still dimensions to the art of manifestation I had not yet understood while I was at Findhorn or at least had not been able to express as clearly as I had wished. For this reason, I eventually took the book out of print, expecting that one day I would be able to do a better job.

As it turned out, for a number of years, I dealt very little with the idea of manifestation, other than continuing to explore it in my own life. It wasn't until 1988 that a church group asked me to give a lecture on positive thinking and manifestation, and I once again began to think about this subject. In that lecture, I first presented some of the ideas in this book. Subsequently, I was asked to do workshops on the subject, and I even developed a course on manifestation that I teach over computers via modems, a kind of electronic correspondence course that anyone with the right equipment anywhere in the world can take simply by calling into the host computer network on which this course is taught. Through these courses, I developed more fully the concepts and techniques that I share with you here.

Essentially, my perspective is that manifestation has much more to do with incarnation—with shaping ourselves and our world—than with acquisition. It is an act of love and sharing with the rest of creation, possessing as all acts of love do as much of giving in it as of getting. Without a sense of passion and presence, it becomes a technique of mindless acquisition, one that dulls our lives rather than enlivening them with spirit.

Manifestation is an act of trust. It is the soul pouring itself out into its world, like a fisherman casting a net to gather in the fish he seeks; with each cast properly made, we will bring what we need to us, but first we must hurl ourselves into the depths without knowing just what lies beneath us.

Chapter Three

A Cosmology of Manifestation

When I begin a class on manifestation, I ask my students to tell their favorite manifestation story. Upon reflection, everyone discovers that he or she has one, even if they have assumed that they have never manifested anything. In one of my classes, one of the participants, Bill, told the following:

One year he sailed solo from Panama to Hawaii. En route, he decided that he wanted to build another boat, a catamaran with traditional Chinese junk sails, which would be easier for him to handle. Such a configuration was very rare, and he wasn't sure just how to build it or how it would sail. While in Maui, he befriended a couple with two small children who themselves had a catamaran. One day they sailed their boats to a cove on the island of Lanai. There his friend showed him blueprints for a boat design he'd been working on, which turned out to be a catamaran with Chinese junk sails!

Discovering that his newfound friend had a similar vision as he did and was offering him help in building the boat of his dreams was an exciting event for Bill, but he knew that the project would take thousands of hours of labor. Before starting on it, he wished he could actually sail a junk-rigged boat to be sure it was what he really wanted.

The next morning he arose early and was fixing himself a cup of tea when a small Chinese junk-rigged boat sailed in to join him and his friend in the bay! The owner of the boat, a California carpenter who had built it himself, then took him out for the day to try the boat out and see if it was what he really wanted to build. At the end of the day, he returned, convinced that a junk-rigged catamaran was the boat he wanted, and he was now ready to build it.

Bill concluded his story saying, "The Californian's boat was the *only* junk-rigged boat I saw in two and a half years of being on the water, and it showed up the morning after we were looking for a solution to getting me some junk experience. At that point the miraculous part of the manifestation receded into the background and three or four thousand hours of intense work took over to make the dream reality."

Bill's story is about a meaningful coincidence, also called a synchronicity, which could be another term for manifestation. You have probably experienced such coincidences in your life, too. What kind of universe enables such things to occur?

Until recently our culture accepted a view of the cosmos in which such coincidences should not or could not happen. There was no place in the clockwork, mechanistic universe portrayed by nineteenth-century science for anything like manifestation, miracles, or magic.

Fortunately, modern science with its explorations into quantum reality, ecology, chaos, and complexity is giving us a very different image of the world than that which had been accepted in the industrialized West even up through the middle of this century.

In order to explore the principles that underlie manifestation, I quite often refer to this new scientific cosmology and draw metaphors from it. There are two reasons for this. I have always had a love for science, born no doubt from having a scientist for a father and an inventor and engineer for a grandfather. Before I embarked on the path of "free-lance mystic," I was working for a degree in molecular chemistry. I chose not to become a practicing scientist, but my love for science continues to this day.

Also, science itself is opening new perceptions of the connections between the physical and the mystical. Over the past two decades, numerous books have been written on the parallels between the worldviews of the mystic and of the quantum physicist and on what might be called the "physics of consciousness." Today, when I use metaphors and images from the physical and biological sciences to express my inner spiritual vision, I feel I am in good company.

This does not mean, however, that I am attempting to describe the working of manifestation in quantum mechanical terms (though physicist F. David Peat has attempted in his book *Synchronicity* to do just that; his book and others that contribute to this discussion are listed in the Bibliography). I am not attempting a *scientific* explanation. The way in which manifestation works may not be open to a purely scientific explanation or description at all. (Then again, it may be, but if so, I am not the one to provide it.)

Nevertheless, since manifestation is part of the universe in which we live, the reasons why it works must relate to how the universe is structured and to the laws that govern it. By looking at what science currently knows about this, we may gain some insights into the principles behind this phenomenon.

Dreams of Fields

The working of manifestation has its foundation in the idea of fields of force or energy. A book in my library called *All That Is Solid Melts into Air* deals with the challenge of the spirit of modernity to traditional philosophical outlooks. I love the title. It particularly captures one aspect of the challenge to our customary worldview. This is the challenge presented by modern physics, whose discoveries show that all that was once considered immutable and solid, even matter itself, is now seen to be patterns of relationship and fields of probability and force.

In *Microcosm,* the economist George Gilder writes, "The central event of the twentieth century is the overthrow of matter. . . . The powers of the mind are everywhere ascendant over the brute force of things." In the first chapter of his book, he gives a succinct overview of the development and implications of quantum mechanical physics, referring to the quantum realm as a realm of information and to the quantum atom as "an atom of information." He proceeds to say, "In the atom of information, this era acquires its definitive symbol. What was once a blank solid is now revealed in part as information; what was once an inert particle now shines with patterns and probabilities." And later he writes, "The move from macrocosm to microcosm can be seen as a progress from a material world composed of blank and inert particles to a radiant domain rich with sparks of informative energy."

Patterns, probabilities, sparks and atoms of information, fields of force—these terms describe a strangely different universe from the one our culture assumed to be true a hundred years ago. All that was solid *has* melted into air, and we now see a universe vastly more energetic, dynamic, and mindlike than we had previously suspected. It is a universe in which a materialist paradigm, and patterns of thought based on materialist logic, can only scratch the surface of reality. Indeed, they often obstruct us from viewing and participating in that reality at a deeper level.

This image of the universe arising from the dynamic interplay of fields of force, a universe rich in possibility and information, is itself not new, though through quantum mechanical physics, chaos theory, micro- and molecular biology, ecology, and the information sciences and computer technologies, we are looking at it in new ways with images and techniques not available to our ancestors. If we substitute the word *presence* or *soul* for the word *field*, and *life* for *energy* or *force*, we actually are very close to the worldview of the ancient mystery and mystical teachings. In this view, everything is alive, and we live in a universe in which we interact on all levels not with inert things but with living presences.

Many spiritual teachings tell of a primal oneness or spirit from which all things emerge. This ancient teaching is paralleled as well by new images from contemporary physics. For example, physicist David Bohm in his book *Wholeness and the Implicate Order* discusses the existence of a primal state, the implicate order, in which everything is enfolded. This order is a wholeness from which the universe unfolds or explicates itself; in turn, each element and object of the universe contains this wholeness, this enfolded order. The totality of the cosmos is enfolded within each of us.

In the enfolded order there is neither time nor space as we know them. At that deep level of wholeness, everything is a part of everything else. Although this description of the universe comes from an interpretation of quantum mechanics, it is the same description that we gain from the literature of mystical experiences.

In modern physics and cosmology, the universe is made up of energy and fields, from which matter is derived. Energy can take any form, while fields are patterns that organize energy into forms. Both energy and fields are hypothesized as arising from a unitary state, perhaps Bohm's implicate or enfolded order. Here we encounter a primal creative trinity, familiar to us already from various religious traditions.

The interplay of energy and fields creates systems, patterns of interconnectedness, interaction, and behavior. Everything we know of might be seen as a system of one kind or another, including ourselves. A system is a way of describing an object or condition holistically.

Some systems process information and energy in ways that enable that system to transcend its present state and grow into new behavior. Given the appropriate energy, the system can repattern and transform itself. Such systems are called "self-organizing." All living creatures are self-organizing systems, but so is the earth itself and the cosmos beyond.

The study of systems, particularly self-organizing ones, has led to the development of new sciences such as the science of dynamics, the science of complex systems, and chaos mathematics. These interrelated sciences also give us a picture of a dynamic, interactive, interconnected universe. One concept that has come from these fields is that of the *attractor*, especially the *strange attractor*. An attractor is not a point in space or a thing like a magnet. Rather it is a nonphysical organizing principle, if you will, describing the end toward which a dynamic system evolves. If that end is a final state, the attractor is called a *point attractor*. If the end is a repetitive, cyclical state, then it is a *cyclical attractor*. If the end, however, is a nonrepetitive pattern, a nonlinear, complex, chaotic pattern, then the attractor is a *strange attractor*.

The idea of the attractor suggests that within chaos is a complex form of order, one that we have not been able to recognize before because we have not had the tools to see it or describe it.

Nonlinear or chaotic systems are profoundly influenced by the conditions that initiate them. The smallest change can have a very large effect. This has become known as the Butterfly Effect. (The name comes from a metaphorical example used to illustrate this phenomenon: that something as seemingly tiny and inconsequential as the flutter of a butterfly's wings can set up a chain of cascading consequences, such as a growing interaction of atmospheric disturbances that eventually could result in a tornado or hurricane many thousands of miles away.)

Research leads scientists to believe that most systems in the universe (certainly those upon which the cosmos depends) are nonlinear, chaotic systems defined by strange attractors. Such systems are indeterminate; that is, their future behavior cannot be predicted with any great accuracy. Thus, unpredictability, chaos, wildness lie at the heart of the universe. We do not live in a predetermined, clockwork, mechanistic cosmos. The door is always open for revelation, emergence, newness, and transformation.

On the other hand, very recent research suggests that while chaotic systems are, well, *chaotic* and essentially unpredictable, they can be affected and to some extent directed. Small systematic changes made into the chaotic system can cause the chaotic element to be reduced or ordered in a new way, giving the system a small shove in a desired direction.

What does all this mean for manifestation? We do not have to be chaos mathematicians or quantum mechanical physicists to use this inner art, but it is important that we begin to revision the universe within which manifestation takes place. The scientific worldview of the last century, which unfortunately is the one with which most people are familiar and which tends to dominate our cultural imagination, posits a world filled with objects and beings separated by time and space; it is a world made up of isolated particles interacting according to mechanistic laws of motion, cause and effect, and so forth.

However modern they seem, ideas of creative visualization, positive thinking, prosperity consciousness—in a way, the whole New Thought movement and its varied offshoots—are all based on this classical scientific worldview, the world of the separated particle. In such a worldview, the phenomenon of manifestation, assuming it is accepted at all, would be seen as something like magnetism, drawing a separate thing, person, or condition to ourselves across space and time. The "magnet" of manifestation pulls to us whatever corresponds to the images and beliefs we hold in our minds.

This raises a number of questions. What is the force or energy that crosses space and time to draw the object of our manifestation toward us? Is it a kind of "psychic" magnetism, whatever that may be?

Furthermore, in this classic worldview, we begin the process separated from that which we wish to manifest. That separation expresses as an awareness of lack. We must somehow, through the strength of our work, creativity, faith, belief, affirmations, or positive thoughts, overcome the obstacles of distance and separation. We must "reach out" and draw what we want to us.

In the worldview of modern physics, that separation may not really exist. We are connected in subtle and important ways with the universe. If we accept David Bohm's notion of an enfolded order, *then we already have that which we wish to attract.* The challenge is not to draw it to us across some distance of space and time, but to explicate and inhabit the pattern that we form with the object of our manifestation. Manifestation, then, is an issue of repatterning and of generating the appropriate and sufficient energy to reorganize our lives into the new pattern we seek. In keeping with the spirit of the Butterfly Effect, if we introduce just the right image or right thought at the right time into the dynamic field of our own being—and hence into the larger field of the world in which our field is enfolded—we can bring about the manifestation we desire. In this dynamic system, the image of what we wish to manifest is the *strange attractor*, the repatterning, organizing principle that shapes the unpredictability of the future into a specific form.

In such a worldview, we do not *acquire* that which we desire; we *become* it.

This idea of fields provides a foundation for a cosmology of manifestation. Upon this foundation are six other related ideas. I call them the six pillars of manifestation. The first three—waves, interrelationship, and co-incarnates—deal with the structure of the cosmos. Like the concept of fields, they reflect the body of the universe. The second three—mind, essence, and unity—relate to the spirit that inhabits or expresses itself through that structure. They reflect the soul of the universe. This body and soul are not two separate things but two aspects of one mystery: one single universal incarnation.

The First Pillar: Waves

When the cry "Surf's up!" is heard on the beaches of southern California and Hawaii, it's a signal to grab your board and head for the waves. When I seek to manifest, I am heading for waves, too, only these are waves of possibility.

In quantum physics, the basic material of the universe—the subatomic matter from which everything is formed—can exist in two states: as a particle or as a wave. This basic stuff is neither one of these two states exclusively but something that encompasses both of them and can express as either.

This "something" cannot be described. We are familiar in ordinary life with waves, like the ocean waves that make surfers so happy. We are also familiar with particles, separate individual things like apples, oranges, Ping-Pong balls, and people. We are not so familiar with something that is both at the same time.

Particles describe a particular location in time and space. A small Celtic cross sits on my desk. That is its location. It is not on my desk and on the table across the room at the same time.

A wave, on the other hand, can fill the room. It is not localized. When I turn my radio on, it does not receive radio waves only when it is on my desk but not when it is on the table. The radio waves are not in a specific spot in my office the way that the Celtic cross is. Wherever I carry the radio, even outside my office, it still receives the broadcast to which I have tuned it.

In quantum physics subatomic matter is called a "wave packet." This term suggests that it is a mixture of both a wave and a particle, in a manner we do not understand. However, this basic stuff is also called "probability." The universe is made up of probability, and the wave state contains all the probable locations that its particle state might occupy.

People are not quantum phenomena, though we are made up of subatomic processes that are quantum phenomena. (There is, in fact, some evidence that consciousness itself may be a quantum state, obeying the same laws as do other quantum phenomena like electrons and photons.) However, if I were to describe myself in my particular state, I would say I am David Spangler, currently sitting in my office in the Pacific Northwest of the United States of America. I am married, and I have four children and four pets.

In my wave state, though, this David Spangler is only one of a nearly infinite number of possible David Spanglers. In my wave state, I have access to a multiplicity of options and possibilities. Some of them are very low on the probability scale; for example, it is highly unlikely that in the next few minutes (or even the next few years, or at any time, for that matter), I will suddenly become President of the United States. However, there are things I could do that would raise that probability (though probably not by much!), such as becoming active in electoral politics. And even though the probability is so low as to approach zero, it is not zero in the wave state. (In fact, I often imagine myself as President in the sense of thinking about the policies I would promote if I held that office.) However improbably, there is still an infinitesimal chance that, in quantum mechanical terms, the wave that represents all the possibilities of my life could "collapse" into my being the President of the United States.

On the other hand, it is far more likely that I will remain here at my desk for the next three hours or so, writing this book, and that I will then get up, not in answer to a summons to the White House but in response to a call for dinner.

Still, it is important to realize that we are not trapped in the "particle" of our history and our habits and the dictates of a purely linear logic in our lives. Other possibilities are available to us as we reach into our wave state and step out of the locality and particularity of our situation. We can deliberately work with the waves of probability to transform our lives. That, in effect, is what the inner art of manifestation is about.

Likewise, when I am in my "particle" state, I am separate from that which I wish to manifest. I do not have it, which is obviously why I want it. However, in the nonlocal wave aspect of my being, the separation does not exist. My consciousness, which is wavelike and quantumlike in its ability to be anywhere or anywhen that it wishes through the power of imagination and visualization, spreads out to include that which I wish to manifest. As particles, we may be separated, but as waves, we are already together.

To say this another way: One of the waves of probability that unfolds from this moment of my life is one that, if it became expressed in a particulate way, would include my possessing, being in relationship with, or experiencing in some manner whatever it is I wish to manifest. Manifestation is the art of making that possibility more probable than it would have been otherwise; in effect, *it is the art of transforming a wave of possibility into a particle of actuality.*

In the wave state, all things are possible, but in the particle state only one or a few things are possible at any given moment. In my wave-consciousness, I can both have and not have the new job I seek to manifest; as a particle, I either have the job or I do not. In the art of manifestation, learning how to accept and work with limits is as important as learning how to tune in to abundance. Both the specificity and the limitations of the particle and the limitlessness of the wave must be understood and appreciated.

The value of understanding the wave state is that it allows me to access the realm of possibility and to expand my horizons of what is possible. Without this experience, I may not be able to envision myself in the kind of particulate reality I would like to have. If I cannot see that new job, for example, as a real possibility, as a reality that I have within myself, and as a potential that I have the capacity to fulfill, then my chances of actually being in that job as a specific particular reality in my life are lessened. By the same token, if I cannot accept or integrate into my life the particularities and specificities of that job and accept its particular limitations, then this, too, can short-circuit the manifestation process.

The Second Pillar: Interrelationship

There is a story that used to make the rounds of environmental groups back in the seventies and eighties. I have also read it in at least two books on ecology, but the authors did not give a reference for it, so perhaps it is apocryphal. At least it illustrates my point, and it is certainly representative of hundreds of other similar stories from the field of environmental studies.

It seems the World Health Organization was attempting to eliminate malaria in a section of Borneo by spraying DDT over native villages. The pesticide was intended to kill off the mosquitoes that carry the disease, and toward this end it succeeded. The incidence of malaria dropped dramatically amongst the population. However, during this same time, it was noticed that the number of cases of plague was rising dramatically. Also, some of the village longhouses (each of which was home to several families) were collapsing as their thatched roofs disintegrated.

Investigation showed that a species of insect lived in the grasses that made up the thatched roofs of the longhouses. Normally, these insects ate these grasses but were in turn eaten by lizards, who themselves were eaten by village cats. This cycle kept both the insect and lizard population in check.

After spraying, the DDT covered the grasses of the roofs and was ingested by the insects, who were not harmed by the chemical. However, DDT concentrates as it moves up the food chain. Thus, the lizards that ate the insects (which had DDT now stored in their bodies) eventually died from DDT poisoning, as did the cats from eating the lizards. As the cats died, rats invaded the villages from the surrounding jungle, bringing with them fleas that carried plague. Also, without the lizards to keep down their population, the insects multiplied unchecked, feasting on and eventually destroying the roofs of the longhouses.

The insects, the lizards, the cats, the rats, the houses, and the villagers had all lived together in an interconnected microecology. They lived together in a *system*. When one element of that system was disturbed, the whole system reacted in a way that was initially unexpected but that could be understood in hindsight.

The idea of systems is particularly explicit in the science of ecology. We are accustomed to thinking of the individual animals and plants that make up a particular environment, but now we are learning to see the whole pattern of interaction between these creatures and the landscape as a thing in itself, an ecosystem.

The old adage of not seeing the forest for the trees is literally true when dealing with ecosystems, for a forest is an ecological unit in itself, made up not only of trees but of many other animals and plants as well. Thus, the controversy over the danger to the spotted owl in the American Pacific Northwest due to logging its habitat can be misleading if we think that just a single species is at risk. The spotted owl is actually an indicator species whose well-being is indicative of the well-being of the forest as a whole and of many other species who live in and "incarnate" the forest. It is the ecosystem that is at risk, not just a single species.

The systems perspective is one of interrelationship; it holds that everything is a system or is part of a system. When we apply this perspective to manifestation, it means that what we seek to manifest is itself a system or part of one, and by manifesting it, we make it become part of the system of who we are. In other words, we invite something that already has its own web of interrelationships to become interconnected with the web of interrelationships that make up our own lives. When this new interrelationship is formed, new information, new patterns, new potentials—a new system—emerge as a result.

This new system may bring with it unexpected consequences. I have always been an ardent fan of board games, for example, and in fact, I have earned part of my living over the years as a game designer. Because of this interest, I collect games. I'm sure when my wife married me, she didn't realize that she was also manifesting a library of several hundred games (not to mention a book library of several thousand volumes—I like to read, too!).

Here is another description of a holistic perspective that takes interrelatedness into account. It is from the introduction to *A Pattern Language,* a book on architecture by Christopher Alexander, Sara Ishikawa, and Murray Silverstein.

"In short, no pattern is an isolated entity. Each pattern can exist in the world, only to the extent that [it] is supported by other patterns: the larger patterns in which it is embedded, the patterns of the same size that surround it, and the smaller patterns which are embedded in it.

"This is a fundamental view of the world. It says that when you build a thing, you cannot merely build that thing in isolation, but must also repair the world around it, and within it, so that the larger world at that one place becomes more coherent, and more whole; and the thing which you make takes its place in the web of nature, as you make it."

We each have a unique pattern. My pattern includes my body, my memories, my thoughts and feelings, my relationships, the place in which I live, the job I do, the systems of which I am a part, and my participation in an ultimate unity.

A pattern is like a wiring diagram. It describes the nature of the relationships and connections I am forming and sustaining in my life. Whenever I seek to manifest something, I am also seeking to change my pattern—the sum total of my interrelationships—to a greater or lesser degree. (Manifesting a toaster will probably not alter my pattern very much, but manifesting a marriage partner certainly will!)

Part of the inner art is learning to be sensitive to the interrelationships represented by systems and patterns and to intuit the possible consequences when my pattern and that of the objective of my manifestation come together.

The Third Pillar: Co-Incarnates

The power of manifestation is not something I possess in isolation from my world. It is a shared power. The more you have of it, the more I have of it, and conversely, the less able you are to manifest, the less able I am to do so. That is the impact of the co-incarnational dimension of our lives.

Individual choice and initiative always have the power to rise above collective inertia. (Otherwise, we would never get anywhere, and many of the great advances of human history would never have been made.) However, none of us lives separate from our common humanity or from the life of the world. When the whole of which we are a part is healthy and vibrant, creative and inspired, then our own creativity, inspiration, health, and vitality are enhanced that much more. It is the difference between swimming against a current and swimming with it.

People can rise above circumstances, and history is filled with examples of people who did just that, but this is not the same as saying that people are separate from their circumstances. Our environment, our social condition, our community, town, neighborhood, ethnic group, and so forth, are all part of what incarnates us. They are part of our extended body. We can change these things, hopefully for the better, but we are not separate from them.

We are accustomed to think of ourselves in singular terms. "I" have the power, and this "I" is a singular entity, a particle. But I am also a wave, to return to my quantum metaphor, and as a wave, I am part of ever-expanding layers of community. Which part of me, the particle or the wave, possesses the power to manifest? My answer is that both do, working together in wholeness. If I deny the wave, I cut off part of that power; if I deny the particle, I cut off part of it, too.

Any conditions that demean or diminish an individual's spirit, imagination, creativity, or will—destroying the particle —or any conditions that enhance selfishness, destroy community, diminish connections and interrelationships, and deny love—destroying the wave—act against the power of manifestation for everyone. On the other hand, manifestation thrives where community and acts of mutual empowerment are present and where the uniqueness and value of the individual are appreciated.

The idea of community can be carried to a deeper level, one that is resonant with Bohm's notion of wholeness. This is that we live in a co-incarnational universe. Everything that is exists because of and in relationship to something else. Each entity's incarnation is more than just its unique configuration, the information it contains and manifests, and the boundaries that keep it distinct. Its incarnation also includes the interrelationships and connections that define its participation within a larger reality. Its incarnation is not just a thing but a pattern that defines how it is embedded in the world. As such, it also is part of the pattern of the incarnation of others.

To be sure, each of us is unique. There is no other David Spangler precisely like me. But what makes me unique is not my name or my physical and psychological makeup. Someone else might have my name (several people do, in fact), might look like me (or be made to look like me, poor chap), and think like I do. But no one else has my particular relationship to my parents, to my wife and children, to my hobbies, to my profession, to my friends, to my environment, or to spirit. These things, which are essential elements of my uniqueness, are part of the pattern of my incarnation. They *are* my incarnation. I call myself a teacher, but if no one ever attended any class I offered or read anything I had written, would I really be a teacher? Those who graciously listen to me help make me a teacher: They *co-incarnate* my reality as a teacher.

We are all co-incarnates. We are all manifesting each other, or perhaps more precisely, we are each contributing to and maintaining the conditions—the total ecology of being—that enables each of us to exist and to unfold.

The individual pattern of a person or thing as formed by its co-incarnates is dynamic. Some aspects of it last for a lifetime; other aspects are fleeting. My parents certainly are co-incarnates of mine, and they will be my parents throughout my life. They will always occupy some portion of the pattern that is myself, although the actual nature of the relationship between us will change over time. On the other hand, a particular job or place of residence may be part of my pattern for only a short time. If I move or take on a new job, the relationship changes. A new set of co-incarnates comes into the pattern.

Can an object be an active co-incarnate? Yes, if it defines who we are and what we do and in some manner shapes or influences our behavior. Remember Archie Bunker's chair in the TV show *All in the Family*? It was sacrosanct. Archie's behavior often revolved around that chair. It became so identified with him that it later was placed in the Smithsonian Institution as an American cultural icon: Daddy's Chair.

An inanimate object becomes actively co-incarnational when our relationship to it is sacramental. Think of all the crosses in the world that Christians venerate and use. An object can be co-incarnational when its function alters our lives, and we become dependent on it in some way. Consider the co-incarnational power of computers or of automobiles.

When we wish to manifest something, then we look to the co-incarnational relationship it forms with us. In the final analysis, that is what we will be manifesting: not the thing or the person but the pattern that that thing or person forms with us.

The Fourth Pillar: Mind

Jim had been diagnosed with lung cancer and was given five months to live. Accepting this prognosis, he began to close out his affairs in preparation for his death. Then one day, a friend mentioned that it was possible to find parking places simply by imagining that one will be there right where you need it. This seemed ridiculous to Jim, but the next time he drove downtown in the city where he lived, he tried it. To his surprise, it worked. He soon found he could manifest a parking place whenever and wherever he wanted, even at peak traffic times in the most congested parts of the city. This experience opened him to the possibilities inherent in the creative power of his imagination, mind, and spirit. He thought that if he could manifest parking spaces, why not something more important, like good health? So he set about to manifest healthy lungs. He did. That was twenty years ago, and he is alive and well today, his cancer fully in remission.

Jim's story is dramatic, but it is not unique. The power of consciousness to affect physical health is well known, but recent research into such disciplines as psychoneuroimmunology (which is the study of the effect of mental and emotional states on the body as a whole and on the nervous and immune systems in particular) and the use of imagery and visualization to improve performance in sports, in business, and in education suggest that this power is more comprehensive than anyone had suspected. The distinctions and boundaries between mind and matter, a legacy of the French philosopher and mathematician René Descartes, are far more permeable and overlapping— far less separating and limiting—than we have been taught.

Caroline, another friend of mine, participated in research in which test subjects like herself had an irritating chemical injected just under the surface of their arms. Depending on the kind of chemical used, an allergic reaction took place, causing wartlike bumps or some other kind of irritation to appear on the skin. The test subjects were then instructed to use any technique they liked, including prayer, meditation, imagery, concentration, or visualization, to make the irritation go away.

Caroline, as well as others in the test, discovered that by focusing her mind on the irritation and willing it to go away, she could heal it. It didn't seem to matter what technique was used; the key element was the directed and focused use of the mind. In fact, by the end of the research project, Caroline had developed the ability to make warts appear and disappear on her arm purely by the use of thought.

In our materialistic and mechanistic culture, we are taught that mind and consciousness are ephemeral, a phenomenon of matter. The mystical and esoteric traditions, on the other hand, reverse this. They say that all matter is a projection of consciousness and that reality is created by thought. In a way, both views are right, for matter and mind alike are reflections or aspects of something else, a more primal substance and process that we may call the universal field of being. It is here, in the internal permutations and interactions of this field, that primal states of mind and matter are transformed from one to the other and back again; it is here that the energy that sustains and creates the universe is generated.

Implicit in this image is that mind permeates everything. Everything is mind, partakes of mind, expresses mind, and is connected by mind. However, in saying this, a clarification is necessary. This primal state of mind is much more than what we normally call "mind." To say that the universe thinks as you and I think is a vast oversimplification, a projection of human experience onto the totality of creation. Our mind is a reflection, not a description, of primal universal mind.

We often use the word *mind* to mean simply "thought" or "intellectualization," and we tend to think of our own individual mind as separate from all others. In this context, manifestation may be seen as a process of using the power of your mind to influence the minds of others.

Yet our mind is more than just the mental content and processes of our rational intellect. As Caroline learned, it includes the functioning of our bodies—in particular, the nervous, endocrine, and immune systems. In fact, all aspects of our bodies contribute to the phenomenon of mind, including our morphological structure, that is, the way we are built. Mind also includes our relationships with the world: It is our memories, our genetic coding, our ancestry, our cultural identity, our dreams of the future, our connections to other living species and to the earth in general.

Furthermore, the universe is a holistic unity, and mind reflects that wholeness. Mind is a "nonlocal" phenomenon, not restricted to a particular place like the brain or body. As anthropologist and cyberneticist Gregory Bateson has pointed out, mind is a pattern—a pattern that connects—and it exists in relationship. It is found not just *within* us but in the spaces *between* us. I may talk about *my* mind, but there is an aspect of mind that is *ours* as well and, as Bateson discusses in his classic book, *Mind and Nature*, part of nature and the larger cosmos. In effect, mind unfolds from and reflects the primal unitive field, the pattern of all the interrelationships that constitute the universe.

This is why I resist descriptions of manifestation as "mind over matter." Mind is a participatory phenomenon, not necessarily a controlling or dominating one. Mind is not "over" matter (nor matter "over" mind). Each shapes and affects the other in a universal dance that creates and dissolves forms and patterns.

Manifestation is the art of transforming these patterns from within. It is the art of repatterning, of changing and fine-tuning the web of relationship and interconnection. It is the art of creating a new tune so that these ancient partners of mind and matter may dance a new dance across the ballroom of the cosmos—or at least through the living rooms of our personal lives.

The Fifth Pillar: Essence

When I was seven years old, my parents and I were living on an American air base in Morocco in North Africa, not far from Casablanca. One day we were driving into that city on a shopping expedition, and I was sitting in the back seat looking out the window and watching a group of Arab women washing their clothes in an irrigation ditch that we were passing. All at once, I felt a strange but not unpleasant sensation in my body, as if I were a balloon and someone were inflating me. Before I had a chance to really examine it and see whether I should be frightened or not, I found myself out of my body, looking down on the car, seeing clearly through its roof as if with X-ray vision. There in the car were my mother and father, and there also was me, still looking out the window!

In the next instant, the car disappeared. I was immersed in a brilliant light that gave way to a succession of images and panoramas that culminated in a vision of floating in space looking down on the spiral curves of our Milky Way galaxy. All of space was filled with a warm golden light, and the galaxy itself pulsed with a life with which I felt totally at one. There was no sense at all of being David Spangler, only of being Life, a life that permeated everything throughout the cosmos.

I seemed to stay in that state of oneness for a very long time, filled with an ecstatic joy. Then, the process seemed to reverse itself. I became David again and saw myself hurtling toward the earth. The next moment, I was once more looking out the window of our car. It seemed as if I had been gone forever, yet the car had hardly moved, and I knew the whole experience had lasted only a few seconds of clock time.

This experience left me with an awareness that beyond the physical world, there are nonphysical or spiritual worlds. These inner realms are not yet dealt with by science, but they have always been part of the mystical and esoteric traditions. Such traditions acknowledge that we are all metaphysically amphibious: We live in more than one dimension at once. We are physical beings, but at the same time we are inhabitants of a spiritual reality that embraces and transcends the physical dimension.

The aspect of us that lives in that spiritual dimension has been given many names, such as *spirit* or *soul*. In the context of manifestation, I call it essence. The idea of essence is a reflection of my own inner experiences, as well as of the many mystical and shamanic traditions that teach that everything has an inner nature. This essence is like a field of energy. It is the specific quality that differentiates one thing from another, even though they may look alike in form and behavior. It is the core identity.

It is easy to visualize the essence of a fellow human being; I can, after all, simply extrapolate from my own personal subjectivity. But unless I am shamanically inclined, I may have difficulty transferring this perception to a chair or an automobile. To speak of a chair as having a unique inner state seems patently ridiculous. Yet I can imagine the "energy" of a chair. Many objects, both human-made and naturally occurring, have a beauty, a grace, a charisma around them that is very appealing. This may be due to their shape, to the processes that went into creating them, and to their functionality. Any psychic worth his or her salt will tell you that objects are also infused with the energy of the people who created them, own them, or use them. Consider, for example, the energy state or essence of a cross or a chalice used to celebrate a High Mass. These are not considered ordinary objects but are imbued with a mystery—a field of energy—appropriate to their sacramental use.

However, it has been my experience that beyond such infusions of quality and energy through use and association, there is still a quality of essence, of nonphysical energy, that exists within every thing that is the *isness* of the thing itself, emerging from its own inner nature and not from its environment.

One way to attune to the essence of that which you wish to manifest is to consider how it is unique. How is it different from other similar objects, for example? It is that uniqueness that will be entering into and impacting upon my life. I am not getting the ideal house. I am getting a particular house that will have its own idiosyncrasies and quirks. I am not marrying the archetypal woman. I am marrying a particular woman who has her own individuality.

Attuning to essence goes hand in hand with recognizing and honoring the differences, the individuality, the uniqueness of everything about us. It reminds us that while our minds create categories and try to fit everything into them, life creates objects and people that are one-of-a-kind—categories in themselves—that will never fit our preconceived notions. To manifest successfully is to accept into our lives that which is different from what we imagined and to be open to and appreciate those differences.

For me, the inner essence of the objects in my world is not a metaphor but a very real concrete experience; it is an aura or emanation that everything possesses. When I seek to manifest something, I am drawing that aura into my life to interact with my own. Learning to attune to and recognize the essence or energy within things expands our sensitivity to our world and further emphasizes that I am incarnating and living in a sea of relationships, not in a quarry of dead objects that I can use any way I like.

The Sixth Pillar: Unity

In 1989, just before Christmas, my family and I were participating in a musical concert put on by a wonderful children's band in Seattle called Tickle Toon Typhoon. Our job was to put on wings and antennae and when the band began to play "Hug Bug," we were to run out from backstage and move through the audience hugging everyone. As this doesn't require a great deal of rehearsing, we had some time on our hands backstage. I had been trying with no luck to find a particular toy as a Christmas present, and this had been on my mind for a couple of days. Knowing there was one specialty store in Seattle that might have it, I went to a pay phone to call them and inquire. As I raised my quarter to put it in the slot, the phone rang. Without thinking, I answered it.

"Hello?" said a woman's voice on the other end.

"Hello," I answered. "Who is this?"

"This is American Eagles hobby store." As it happened, this was the very store I was intending to call! "I was just about to call you!" I blurted out in amazement.

"Really?" the lady replied. "That's funny. I thought I heard the phone ring. There was no one on the line, and I was about to hang up when you said hello!"

This was an incredible coincidence. No one backstage had used the phone in the half hour or so I had been there, and it was highly unlikely that any of the other parents or children would have called that particular store, which specialized in military models and war games. Further, it was a pay phone, and I had not yet put any money into it. I was just about to do so when the phone rang. Nor had the lady in the store dialed her phone; she had simply picked it up, thinking she had heard it ring.

This event was a coincidence, but it was a *meaningful* coincidence. It corresponded to the specific thought I had of calling a particular hobby store. Such meaningful coincidences were called synchronicities by Carl Jung. I think of manifestation as a controlled or invoked synchronicity.

Synchronicities are the outward expression of an underlying

order or pattern within or beneath all the manifestations of the cosmos. They are an expression of the fundamental unity, the interconnectedness, the interrelatedness, the co-incarnatedness of creation. Synchronicities are possible because the dimensions of space and time that normally separate objects and events are subsumed into a deeper pattern of interpenetration and interaction. And so we return to the primal state David Bohm called the enfolded or implicate order, with which this chapter began.

By the way, my story of the magical phone call from the hobby shop is an excellent example of synchronicity, but as it turned out, not such a good one of manifestation: They did not have the model I was looking for!

The Universe of Manifestation

Manifestation is possible because we live in a cosmos that at its deepest level is made up of relationships unfolding out of a state of primal unity. Everything unfolds in a unique way but retains a connection to the unified state. Everything unfolds with the help of relationships with other, equally unfolding entities. We are all in one degree or another co-incarnates of each other.

We think of owning and possessing, of having things and people in our environment. Yet all these things and people are part of the pattern—the "wide body"—of our incarnation. They are our extended body, as important to the uniqueness and expression of our being as our particular physical body may be. We are defined, expanded, limited, and structured by our possessions and relationships. They form a metaphysical "skin" that establishes at any moment just where and what our particular boundaries may be.

Therefore, when we manifest something or someone, we are

affecting that boundary; we are expanding, shrinking, or in some way altering that "skin." We are incarnating ourselves and, by co-incarnational extension, the rest of the world as well. Hence, all manifestation is an act of co-incarnation disguised as an act of acquisition.

By thinking of manifestation as simple acquisition, I can maintain a perspective of being separate from my world and separate from the things I own; I can take a superior stance to both. However, when I learn to think and perceive from the perspective of incarnation and relationship, then I see myself as a participant in a co-creative dance with life, neither fully subject nor object but, like the wave/particle duality of light, something that is a bit of each and more than either.

Manifestation is an act of participation, of deepening. The more I can enter into the communion and community of my world, the more manifestation will work for me. This means that manifestation is also an expression of those qualities that normally deepen and enrich relationships: love, compassion, caring, empowerment, and the honoring of difference.

The world of the physicist and the world of the mystic are coming closer and closer together. They may or may not merge, but even running parallel, they both point to a universe that is more unified, interactive, interdependent, participatory, and ecological than mechanical, clockwork, or materialistic. To see manifestation only as a way of wielding mental powers of magnetic attraction and influence over the environment is to remain caught in an older paradigm.

Rather, as the six pillars suggest, we must see ourselves as co-manifestors—partners in manifestation—all engaged in the primal act of unfoldment and emergence. Each act of manifestation may be directed toward a specific outcome, but it also contributes to the greater manifestation of the wholeness, love, compassion, and creativity of the primal source from which we all come.

There is another important point. When we think about what we manifest, we usually think in terms of objects, persons, opportunities, or resources. However, once these things become part of our lives, they become aspects of the pattern we call ourselves. They may be separate from us physically, but they are part of the total environmental, physical, psychological, and spiritual pattern that defines us. They are outer reflections of inner states and realities.

In all our acts of manifestation, we are really only manifesting a new aspect of ourselves. We are giving our lives a new shape. We are the primary object of our manifestation.

Chapter Four

The Energy of Miracles

Merrily, my wife's sister, called one day and in the course of the conversation mentioned that she had been investigating Native American shamanic and healing practices. She had gone to see a woman who was trained in shamanic healing and counseling who told her that for her, the elk was a totem animal who would be particularly strong in bringing power and healing into her life. Unfortunately, Merrily felt no connection with elks at all, and she was wondering what to do about it.

The next day after that phone call, a colleague of mine came to visit with my wife and me after having spent a week in New Mexico interviewing Native American medicine people. As he was unpacking, he held up a narrow object wrapped in cloth. "This is interesting," he said, as he unwrapped it to show us. It was a dry curved bone. "Just before I got on the plane to come here to see you, the man whom I had been visiting gave me this. It is the rib bone of an elk. It has been used as a power object for attuning to the elk spirit. He said he felt like I should have it, though he didn't know why. So I brought it with me."

I immediately told him of my sister-in-law's phone call, and he said, "Well, obviously this is meant for her." The next day the elk bone was on its way to my sister-in-law via UPS.

This is a manifestation that just happened. There was no preparation, no technique involved, not even a conscious effort to try to manifest something (and if there had been, I'm sure an elk bone would not have been the first thing to spring to her mind!). My sister-in-law simply voiced a question about how she might improve her attunement to the spirit of the elk.

Here is another story. Vivienne had gone with her young son for a summer retreat on the Scottish island of Iona, a place rich in spirit and history that has long been a place of spiritual pilgrimage. She had been given use of a small house on the beach, and every day her son and a friend he had met went and played in the dunes.

In raising her son, Vivienne had not allowed him to have any violent toys, so in spite of his entreaties, Timothy had never owned any toy guns (though this had not stopped him from making them out of sticks or other things he found).

The third day they were there, Timothy and his friend had gone off to play in the dunes. While running along a ridge of gravelly sand and earth, Timothy tripped over a root and fell, rolling down the sandy hill. He landed unhurt, but his hand fell into a deserted rabbit hole in the side of the hill. As he lay there catching his breath, he realized that his fingers were touching something hard and interesting. Calling his friend over, they dug into the hole and discovered to their absolute delight two toy rifles that had been hidden in it!

Excitedly, the two boys showed their discoveries to Vivienne, Timothy saying to her, "Look, Mom, I manifested them!" As she told me later with a laugh, "What was I to say? I had been teaching him about manifestation, and here he came up with these two toy guns! I could hardly say he had to put them back!" So the boys played happily for two weeks on the beach with their treasures, and then, when it was time to leave, they carefully replaced the toys in the hole where they had found them.

Coincidences and Miracles

Both these stories illustrate coincidences, which are forms of unconscious or unintentional manifestation. For the people involved, they were little miracles that affirmed that they were connected to creation in subtle and wonderful ways. Feeling this connection, we can also feel empowered in our lives, as if we have discovered a credit card that lets us draw on a fabulous bank account.

Not all coincidences are as notable as the two I described. Most are of the common garden variety. You think of a friend, and she calls unexpectedly a moment later. You walk into a store, and there are exactly the earrings you are looking for for your wife. An unexpected bill comes in the mail, but so does an equally unexpected insurance payment that just pays the amount of the bill. A car pulls out from the curb just as you are looking for a parking place.

Experiences like these are actually so common that we probably overlook them most of the time, classifying them, if we think of them at all, as simply "luck."

Yet all coincidences are kissing cousins to miracles. Both represent a mystery that alters our reality in small or large ways. Miracles and coincidences are both wonderful; they are full of wonder. (In fact, the word *miracle* comes from a Latin root, *mirus*, meaning "wonderful.")

I do not believe life itself qualifies miracles into "important" ones and "trivial" ones. Even the smallest miracle, moment of coincidence, or synchronicity can lead us into a whole new way of thinking and behaving, with life-transforming effects. Remember my story of Jim in the last chapter? Something as mundane and simple as manifesting a parking place became the key to miraculously healing himself of cancer.

The sense of connectedness that a coincidence, a synchronicity, a manifestation, or a miracle can bring enlarges us. It expands our perception of our world, allowing us to see more deeply into a reality that lies behind the surface of things. Such a perception can also make us more willing and able to connect and attune to the people and things in our world and to the spirit that lies behind them. It releases a delightful, transforming, and creative energy into our lives. It can change forever our sense of who we are and the role we play in the world.

Yet the question remains: Why do such things happen? Is it a cosmic whim? Is it divine favor, a reward for good deeds? Is it an expression of the self-organizing, patterning, holistic, emergent nature of creation? Is it some occult power within us? Is it luck?

Is there an energy or a condition that gives birth to miracles great and small? If so, is it not this energy that we seek to utilize in the inner art of manifestation?

Exploring the Source of Manifestation

My understanding and teaching about manifestation is based on experience rather than on theory. It comes from the simple expedient of paying attention to coincidences and synchronicities when they happen, of seeing just what they feel like in my body and in the more subtle ranges of my being. It comes from paying attention to what happens when a manifestation is happening or has happened and then trying to replicate it.

To illustrate what I mean, I want to tell you two more manifestation stories.

Once I was driving home from Seattle. My day had not been going well. I had felt irritable in the morning, and as the day wore on, I did nothing to alter my mood. Indeed it got worse and worse until by the time I was heading home, I was fuming inside, enjoying a fine moment of rage and indulging my anger with considerable gusto.

Crossing the bridge across Lake Washington that separates Bellevue and the eastside communities where I live from Seattle itself, I said to myself, "I'm so angry, I could smash glass!" In my mind's eye, I pictured myself with a hammer breaking up panes of glass with great glee.

At that moment there was a loud crash, and the front windshield of my car cracked, nearly shattering. At exactly the same moment I had thought about breaking glass, a passing truck had thrown back a good-sized rock that smashed my window. The shock of it immediately dispersed my anger. Then, looking at the spiderweb of cracks running all over the windshield, I had to laugh. This manifestation had been too literal for my taste!

Manifestation is often explained by saying that our thoughts create our reality. The Book of Proverbs in the Bible says it succinctly: "As he thinketh in his heart, so is he."

In this experience, my broken windshield certainly corresponded to the thought I had had at the moment it was shattered by the rock. The clarity of my image and the angry energy behind it had transcended a barrier between imagination and reality. My thinking certainly seemed to have created my reality.

However, the idea that we create our reality by our thoughts has always seemed simplistic to me. What kind of thinking is effective in this regard? Is it the everyday flow of images and thoughts that we all experience? Does our stream of consciousness have the power to turn the millstones of our reality?

Is it thought plus strong emotion? While not normally given to rages, I have certainly experienced my share of them, complete with angry thoughts of rampage and mayhem. Yet none of those thoughts has ever become real (thank goodness!). In fact, my reality rarely conforms just to what I think or to strong emotions I may be feeling.

This is a good thing. Imagine the panoply of images, fears, worries, desires, daydreams, fantasies, feelings, and thoughts that parade through our heads on a normal day. Would you want all of them translated into reality? And what about on an abnormal day, a day of exceptional stress or pressure? I, for one, am thankful that our everyday thoughts do not have the power to manifest or to shape our reality, at least not directly.

Later that evening, I meditated upon my experience with the broken windshield and sought to understand it more deeply. Not that I was looking for any hidden meanings. I felt I understood pretty clearly what the message had been: Pay attention to the moods I get into because there are occasions when thoughts do influence what happens. This is especially true if, like myself, you have been working to align with the forces of manifestation.

What I was intent on reviewing was just what had happened inwardly for me at the moment just before and when the rock struck. I realized that there had been a sensation of a shift, as if for one moment I were inhabiting two realities at once. There was a feeling of singularity, as if everything had come together in a dimensionless point. It was a feeling of clarity and focus, not of anything in particular but of beingness itself.

I realized that for a split second, my whole sense of reality had been heightened and loosened; that it had become more energized, not with anger or with any other emotion but with a primal energy that in fact was very joyous and delightful. I was surprised at finding at the heart of my moment of anger, a joy and a playfulness.

Pursuing this feeling in my meditation, I remembered that as I drove onto the bridge, being fully aware of my anger and that there was no real reason for it except that I had allowed myself to get into a bad mood and had been interpreting everything that happened to me during the day as being irritating and unwanted, I felt a choice. I knew I could let the anger go because it was not very deeply rooted in me, or I could continue it. I chose the latter, but now I was feeling the anger as a kind of play. It was just as intense as it had been before, but its quality had changed. I was angry through a choice. I was deliberately being angry for the experience of it, and there was a sense of delight in seeing what images came out of it. I was recognizing myself—not anything or anyone in my environment—as its source, and I was owning my anger in a peculiarly playful way. There was a wonderful sense of power and release in my image of lifting a hammer and smashing piles of glass over and over . . . and then something shifted, which I felt in my body like an invisible wave passing through me. The reality of the breaking glass and the reality of driving the car seemed to coexist for a moment and then—the rock struck, the windshield shattered, and reality seemed to collapse back into its normal firm, solid character.

In fact, as I reflected on this, I realized that what I had experienced in that short burst of time was metaphorically like the collapse of a wave function in quantum mechanics. For a moment, I had raised my energy to where I entered something analogous to a wave state, in which reality is smeared and all possibilities are present, though not in equal degrees of probability. Then the wave state collapsed, carrying into reality my predominant thought of breaking glass, which manifested itself in the shattered windshield.

What was significant to me, though, was that the energy that seemed to heighten the moment in that way was not my anger but an energy of playfulness coupled with the power of fully acknowledging myself as the source and owner of what I was experiencing.

Some weeks after this, I had another experience of unexpected manifestation that fortunately was much more benign. I have a friend in England, John Matthews, who is a Celtic scholar, prolific author, and a world authority on the legends and stories of King Arthur, the Holy Grail, Robin Hood, and other legends of the Greenwood. We are both devoted fans of the television series *Star Trek: The Next Generation*, *Deep Space Nine*, and *Voyager*. We both have a collection of toy Star Trek characters like Spock, Jean-Luc Picard, Whorf, Data, and others.

Some years back, the company that makes these figures released one for Deanna Troi, the half-human, half-alien telepathic psychologist and counselor for the starship *Enterprise*. As the only female figure in the set at the time, it quickly became a collector's item, especially as the company was releasing only a few of them at a time. Knowing that John wanted one of these (as did I), I combed the local toy stores trying to find two of them. I had no luck. Toys "R" Us, the national toy chain, was my best prospect, but they said there was a long waiting list for this figure and that it would be months before one would become available because the company was making so few of them.

On a chance, I called my parents and asked if they would see if Deanna was available in any of the toy stores where they lived. However, the next day, my father called back to say not only that this figure was not available but that as far as any of the buyers for the stores knew, it never would be available. The manufacturing company, he had been told, had decided to sell the toy only through specialty magazines and catalogs that catered to collectors of science fiction memorabilia. At this point I gave up and stopped thinking about it. I simply released the idea of these toy figures.

Two days later, I was sitting in my office working. I happened to glance up to where I keep my collection of Star Trek figures, and the image of the Deanna Troi toy flashed into my mind. As it did so, I felt a curious sensation of energy shifting within me and around me. Without really thinking about it, I said out loud, "I am going to manifest this thing!" As I said this, I felt as if I were in a very open space, as if the walls of my office had receded into infinity. This was not a visual experience, only a sense of being in an enormous, even limitless presence. Then the sensation stopped and all was normal again. I went back to my work and completely forgot about it.

Three hours later my phone rang, and it was my father. "The most interesting thing just happened to me," he said. "I woke up this morning feeling under the weather, so I decided to stay in bed. Then about three hours ago, I had a sudden impulse to call the local Wal-Mart store and ask about that toy you were looking for. The lady I spoke to said she had just that moment finished unpacking a shipment of Star Trek toys and was holding a Deanna Troi figure in her hand even as we spoke. She said she could hold it for me for an hour before she had to put it on the shelves.

"So," he continued, "I hopped in the car and drove right over; took me about forty minutes because it's on the other side of town, but when I got there, she still was saving the toy for me. Then she asked if I would like to see any of the other figures. I was curious, so I said sure. She took me down the aisle to where these toys were on display, and guess what? There was another Deanna Troi figure, hanging right there! The saleslady had no idea where it had come from, since she had unpacked the box and had only seen the one she had already given me. So I got both of them and came right home and called you up. You did say you wanted two, didn't you?"

In reflecting on this experience later, I realized that the

sense of shifting and heightening I felt was that same feeling of having stepped out of my normal reality or into a space between realities that I had felt just before the rock shattered my windshield. Of course, physically I didn't go anywhere, but my sense of presence had expanded into a place where reality seemed larger and looser. It was as if reality were a latticework whose strands normally were woven into a tight mesh, but in that moment the strands loosened and pulled apart, allowing space to appear within the mesh.

Furthermore, in this instance I was not experiencing any particular emotion. I had been quietly working, not even thinking about the Star Trek figures until I happened to see my collection on my bookshelf. There had been no rage, no desire, no affirmations. What there was, though, was a strong sense of being present. I had been focused upon my work, and I was feeling very present to myself, very much in the moment, very owning and accepting of my own being.

Yet this was also a common link with the bridge experience, for then, too, I had felt very present. In that moment when I knew I could alter my mood and that I was making a choice, I was deeply aware of my own presence. That was a more powerful feeling even than the anger. The latter was simply an emotion, while the former, the sense of presence, was the energy of my whole being focused like sunlight through a lens or, to use a different image, embracing my reality in a seamless and unconditioned way.

And in both cases, there was an underlying sense of playfulness, humor, and delight.

Since then I have noticed a similar sense of presence at other times when I have experienced a successful manifestation. This leads me to look upon presence itself as the powerful energy that allows manifestation to happen. It is the energy of miracles. But what exactly is presence?

Presence

By presence I do not mean some additional mystical part of ourselves, separate from the body or the mind, the soul or the spirit. Our beingness exists over a wide range of experiences, forms, and conditions, from the highly specific density, shape, and structure of our bodies to the universality and unity of the enfolded order or, if you wish, of the mystery and oneness of the sacred. Presence is a moment when all ranges are present, or when we are experiencing the wholeness of the spectrum rather than the characteristics of just one of the ranges. It is a moment —a condition—when the totality of our existence synergizes and blends with our world, expanding the ranges of the reality we inhabit as well. And it does so through attunement, through weaving itself gracefully into our world.

To use my earlier image, the energy of presence widens and opens the latticed mesh of our reality not by opposing or challenging it but by becoming part of it, blending with it, and through its own expandedness, expanding the mesh as a whole. Then there is space, there is openness, there is a potential for something new to emerge, for reality to shift, and for miracles to happen.

Because presence represents our holistic self (body, psyche, soul, spirit, and connections), it is not simply a private condition but a shared state, a co-creative, co-incarnational state.

When I think of the different ways people can manifest, I see presence at work in each of them.

Do I manifest through prayer? Prayer is being wholly present to the sacred, fully and joyously attentive to the divine, so that the divine can be fully present to you and the presence of the sacred is with you.

Do I manifest through visualization and affirmation? At their best, these techniques draw me wholly into the presence of that which I seek to manifest, and its presence into me. I am present to it; I am attentive to it, and out of that presence, energy flows.

Is it thought that creates my reality? Only inasmuch as a thought or a feeling recollects my scattered parts and makes me present to my reality, so that my reality and my presence become one.

But a thought or a feeling, a physical sensation or a mystical experience, a clear intent or a strong need—or a combination of any or all of these—can be the trigger that draws our scattered parts together into a wholeness. For that moment, we are the whole spectrum of our possibilities and realities, not just one or two of them. For that moment, we are wholly present and in presence.

Four Energies

As I meditated upon this idea of presence over time, seeking to clarify just what it was and what was happening when I entered into a state of attunement as part of a manifestation project, I began to see that when I felt presence, it seemed to include a synergy of four other energies.

The first of these I called the kinetic energy of my own life. This is the momentum and direction of my identity. It is the pattern I have created and am creating that defines me and my relationships with life. It is made up of my habits, my aspirations, my physical dispositions, my attitudes and thoughts, my beliefs, and so forth.

This dynamic field of personal energy that we all have conserves the reality we are familiar with. When new experiences, new energies, new possibilities engage with us, this field will seek to appropriate and shape them so that they conform to its momentum and direction. On the whole, this is good, for it maintains consistency. But when we wish to change or when we wish to manifest, we may need to expand and loosen up this field so that new possibilities can enter and give us a new direction.

Taken all by itself, this energy may resist the manifestation of anything that is not congruent with it. On the other hand, it can enhance a manifestation if it shares its general direction and intent.

For example, in the story of Merrily's manifestation, the interest in shamanic practices, the image of the elk, the desire to explore a different kind of attunement than she had ever tried before, all represented a part of herself moving in a particular way, seeking to emerge into a new perspective of the world, a new sense of her own identity, a new relationship with spirit, and developing a momentum in that direction.

This momentum, which generally was toward living a more enlightened and attuned life, had been built up over years. It had been nurtured physically through a regime of diet, exercise, and physical activity. It had been cultivated through relationships and connections with people, places, and objects that shared and supported her intent, as well as through the self-transcending discipline and joy of raising a family. It had been energized and clarified by her spiritual practices and her inner work to align more clearly and fully with her soul and with the sacred.

In short, there was a flow in her life that had self-organizing properties. It was the strange attractor of a desired potential reality, and over years of work, it had accumulated a great deal of energy. Into the field of its influence dropped the desire to use shamanic attunement as another way of inner exploration and expansion, and out popped an elk bone!

A second flavor of energy I discerned in presence was one that arose from all the connections I make in life and generally from the web of life itself. Call this web the community of co-incarnates, known and unknown. As I experienced it, this energy generally seeks to enhance both the experience of diversity and individualization on the one hand and the experience of connectedness on the other. It is like the energy of the Musketeers: All for One and One for All. It is also an energy of synergy, where the whole is more than the sum of its parts and where both the whole and its parts work for their mutual well-being.

In terms of manifestation, using my own energy and intent as a template, this web would create within itself a matching configuration made up of a combination of people, events, connections, and the like that would serve the nature of what I was manifesting.

Merrily's elk bone did not just drop in front of her from thin air, nor did my windshield shatter of its own accord with nothing striking it. In both cases a combination of people and events brought the manifestation into being. In Merrily's case, an English colleague of mine, a Native American shaman, an elk bone, my wife, and I all connected at appropriate moments and in appropriate ways, without any advance planning or formal intent, to create a configuration that could produce something Merrily could use to satisfy her intent. Likewise, in the case of my windshield, a good-sized stone on the bridge was run over by a good-sized truck, giving it just the right velocity and trajectory to break the glass, and we all had to be traveling at just the right speed and timing with respect to each other for it to happen.

This combining and recombining of elements within my personal field of energy or that of the co-incarnational web in order to give an image or desire a push over into reality seemed itself to draw upon a third energy. This I call the creativity inherent in any system. It is the energy that inspires and fuels growth, that seeks unfoldment, that rearranges and recombines in order to find new ways of expressing itself. This is the dynamic flow within any system. It does not work so much to maintain the system as to explore the possibilities of what the system can do *without transforming itself*. I emphasize the latter point.

So, for example, an artist draws upon her creativity to paint or to compose music and will seek to develop and enhance her talent to do so; what she will not seek to do is to alter her identity as an artist to become something else, like a traffic cop or a computer programmer. I experience this energy as emerging from and representing our level of essence, the core of our identity. It acts to extend and develop our identity while still preserving its essential character.

This energy is important in manifestation, for all expressions of the inner art are fundamentally creative. You are seeking to create something new in your life. Yet while your manifestation will bring change if only by adding something new to your life, it will not necessarily bring transformation.

Transformation comes from the addition of the fourth energy I could discern in the makeup of presence. This is an energy that derives from the unity of all things. It transcends boundaries because it is the same on both sides. Whether I am an artist, a traffic cop, or a computer programmer does not matter in the presence of this energy, since none of these professions is closer to this unity than any other. This is an energy of pure being. I call it love.

This energy truly opens up our identities and our realities to new possibilities. It is like grace. It is the spirit in which all things are made new. In it, I am not tied to any particular history nor to any particular momentum. It is a spirit of playfulness, a spirit of delight and wonderment, a spirit of discovery, exploration, and unconditioned power. It is not striving to be any particular thing, for it is all things. This makes it the essence of abundance.

In meditation, when I touch into this state, it has another

characteristic as well. It seems pregnant. It seems filled with an infinity of potentials, all of which it wishes to reveal.

In my own imagination I see this energy as the spirit of emergence that lies behind the forces of chaos, complexity, and self-organization that, according to the new directions in physics and cosmology, are creating the universe we live in all the time. It is the spirit of manifestation.

The Boiling of Reality

Over time, I used this idea of presence and these four energies as the focus of a series of meditations and inner workings on manifestation. In so doing, I drew upon the experiences I had had with various manifestations, such as I have been describing. Out of this work came several images that deeply influenced the way I think about and teach manifestation.

One image that came to me I called the "boiling of reality."

Imagine putting a lot of salt into a cup of cold water. Some of it dissolves, but most of it sits there on the bottom of the cup. Now you heat the water in the cup. As the water temperature rises and heat imparts its energy to all the molecules in this solution, the chemical bonds that bind the salt into a crystalline form begin to weaken and stretch. As the water gets still hotter, these bonds finally break, and the salt dissolves. If you then cool the water back down carefully, you end up with a supersaturated solution. There is no pile of salt, for it has all dissolved. But actually there is more salt dissolved in the water than should be there. It is an unstable situation. By adding a few salt crystals to it, they become seeds around which the dissolved salt can recrystallize and then precipitate out of the water. Once again you have a pile of salt in your cup.

Your reality is like that solution. It contains myriad possibilities, some of which have crystallized out into the world you know and the life you lead. But when energy is applied, whether from the momentum of your own desires, from the co-incarnational web you share with others, from a creative energy within you, or from a transpersonal spirit of transformation and grace, this reality becomes heightened and more energetic. It metaphorically boils. The crystals dissolve, and reality loosens and becomes more open. A full spectrum of beingness and creativity connects with the finite moment and renders it open and attuned to the infinite. You experience this openness—this boundary between the finite and the infinite, the potential and the real, the enfolded and the unfolded orders—as presence. From the power of this presence, manifestations emerge and miracles are born.

All miracles big and little, from grand transformations to minor coincidences, occur when our reality has boiled and all our normal perceptions, expectations, habits, histories, and futures have dissolved into solution, their bonds upon our consciousness and spirit loosened and broken. Into this moment of supersaturated potentiality, containing more of infinite possibility than it normally can, drops an image—a reality seed, a particular possibility—and everything precipitates out again, back into normality, back into the everyday rush of time and space. But it does so with a difference, for this reality is now shaped by the seed that triggered the precipitation.

The metaphor of this image of boiling reality pointed me to a key element in understanding the energy of miracles and the process of manifestation. This was the vitality or energy contained in our experience of reality. How constricted was it or how dancing and energetic was it? How easily could my reality be boiled?

I came away from these meditations with an image. It is not

thought that creates our reality. It is presence that creates reality. The more vitality inherent in my experience of reality, the more that reality can respond to that presence and open up to receive and embody the energy of miracles and the spirit of manifestation.

Chapter Five

Reality Vitality:
A Manifestation Fitness
Program

The success of any specific manifestation project rests on the capacity of your current reality to change. It is affected by the vitality of your reality. To enhance this vitality and to bring into your life the kind of energy, attitudes, and connections that support manifestation, I offer a manifestation fitness program.

This represents something you can do all the time, not just when you are engaging in a specific manifestation project. In fact, the object of the inner art is not just to manifest specific objectives now and again, but to be mindful about how you are expressing your creative energy all the time. It is a way to enhance the general flow of manifestation through your life.

For there is never a time when you are not manifesting something, even if it is only the same old habits and lifestyles that you are already familiar with. Your reality is continually bootstrapping itself or giving birth to itself.

This being the case, why not manifest in ways that empower you, give vitality and possibility to your life, and allow you to unfold and prosper? Why not make the reality-generating process within you a mindful and attuned one?

Also, we do not manifest in private but as part of a great collective life. The more you can fill your life with the energy of miracles, the more that energy passes on to others and into the world at large. The more the collective reality is heightened and attuned to its higher potentials, the more you are individually empowered. Reality vitality can be a slogan for everyone!

Is your reality vital? Is it alive and dancing with the energy to translate possibility into actuality, to effect change, to take on a new shape? Is it a reality that supports manifestation? For all manifestation, no matter how trivial, whether it's manifesting a job or a spouse or manifesting a toaster or a car, is a shift of your reality. Big shift or little shift, it is still the same process and draws on the energy of presence to accomplish its aims.

With that in mind, here are some suggested elements of a manifestation fitness program. With some personal reflection, I am sure you can add to this list for your specific circumstances.

Body

All manifestation ultimately must become physical or embodied in some manner. Otherwise it remains abstract or imaginal, a potential rather than a reality. The whole notion of manifestation implies a physical or tangible expression. For this reason, attunement to the physical realm is obviously important.

A person can have a vibrant and powerful inner presence and be a powerful manifestor and still not be well or whole physically; on the other hand, it is easier if your presence is supported by an energetic and healthy body. Your physical body and its energy is a foundation for your actions. It is the instrumentality through which your ideas and plans are carried into action. Many people have good ideas but lack follow-through because they just don't have the energy for it.

Diet, exercise, and whatever else we do to honor and nurture our physical bodies cannot fail to help build a foundation for the inner art of manifestation. Part of a good manifestation fitness program is a good physical fitness program.

I know from experience how the physical body can affect manifestation. As a writer, I spend a lot of time sitting every day, and I have never been keen on exercising as a daily discipline. When I am writing or studying, I can become so concentrated that I forget to move about periodically. So five or six hours later, I end up with a sore back and fatigue, chiding myself for being so neglectful of my physical state. Further, being sedentary, I gain weight if I do not watch my diet or exercise. When I am not mindful of these things, my physical system becomes sluggish. Then the flow of energy through my being feels more like thick syrup than a sparkling dynamic stream. Everything begins to bog down around me. Where normally I am quite good at manifesting, when I am neglectful of my physical state, manifestation slows down and mirrors the sluggishness of my physical energy.

I have found that this sluggishness will begin to disappear and my energy quicken very rapidly as soon as I begin to pay attention to my body again, even before renewing any exercise program. The willingness to be present to body states and give them attention sets energy into motion. If I am physically handicapped or ill, I can still be energized through any effort I make to be in my body in as accepting and whole a way as I can manage at the time. It is the willingness and the act of honoring the physical level through some kind of action, however limited, that uncorks the flow.

When your body is depleted and your energy is low, it is easier to feel discouraged and depressed. In fact, many states of depression are caused by organic rather than psychological causes; they may be rooted in a poor diet, lack of exercise, or simple fatigue. Keeping your physical energy as vital as you can is an important way to maintain positive presence.

Visualization and the use of imagination is a key element in manifestation. However, what gives a visualization power is your ability to ground it in your sensory experience. It's one thing to think about an orange and something else again to visualize it by drawing on physical sensations, imagining its shape, its color, its odor, its taste, its smell, and the feel of juice filling your mouth as you bite into an orange slice. The body provides both physical memories and felt senses that can ground and give depth and greater meaning or reality to subjective images and feelings.

Centering is also important. Feeling a center in our lives gives us balance; it enables us to shift patterns quickly and easily if we have to. One way to cultivate the sense of centeredness is through our bodies. Our bodies have a natural center of gravity in the pelvis. By focusing our attention in that area and feeling our energy move out from there, we can experience being centered in a physical way, which can be an inner model for being centered in psychological ways. There are various forms of bodywork and disciplines, like aikido and tai chi, that can train a person in physical and psychological centeredness.

The body is also an instrument of attunement to the world around you. The more vital it is, the more sensitive this attunement can be. When your senses are clear and open, you can connect with your world more fully through them. You are more of a participant—more of a wave—and less isolated in your particularity.

This attunement extends into subtle areas as well. Have you ever been with someone who is depressed or entered a place that has recently seen conflict? Even without knowing anything of the history of that person or place, you can often feel the disharmony in your body. Parts of you will tighten up or feel stress. Alternatively, you can be with a joyous loving person or walk into a place of calmness and quiet, and you can feel your body relaxing or becoming energized.

When evaluating a particular manifestation project, how your body feels when you contemplate your objective can be a good indication of whether you should pursue it. There are times when my mind or my emotions want something but my body is responding with a feeling of tension or a loss of energy, a "gut feeling" that something is not right. I can go into a bookstore and run my hand over a shelf of books and know immediately by a physical response just which book I would enjoy or benefit from reading. Likewise, I can be attracted to a book by its cover or subject matter, but when I pick it up, I may feel a sudden drop in my energy, a sense of physical droopiness, that tells me that this is not really a book I would enjoy.

Paying attention to the felt sense that your body may have about something or someone is a vital way of gaining information of use in your manifestation. You may, for example, feel a physical pull toward a place or a person that, if honored, leads you to make a contact that turns out to be very helpful in fulfilling your objective.

The healthier and more vital your body is, and the more you honor and attune to that part of your consciousness that is centered in the body, the more useful an instrument of insight your body becomes.

There are innumerable resources available to help us improve our physical lives through diet, exercise, and bodywork to relieve tensions and energy locked in habitual muscle patterns. Anything you do that helps your body be more healthy and vital will improve your ability to manifest. In fact, you can do your exercises in the name of your manifestation. ("These twenty-five push-ups are on behalf of that new washing machine I want to manifest!") By linking an action with the presence you wish to manifest, you give it energy.

Your body is the energetic foundation for your manifestation. Keep its energy and health as high and vital as you can, and see it as your ally in pursuing the inner art.

Rhythm

Rhythm is another important consideration. Many of us lead harried and hurried lives. Each day brings new demands. We become pulled in several different directions. It becomes difficult to maintain any kind of rhythm or schedule. One day we eat breakfast, the next day we are in a hurry, so we don't. We sleep eight hours one night, four hours the next. We become dispersed and scattered; our center does not hold.

Rhythm is one of the secrets of creative power. The cosmos dances to rhythm. Rhythm sets up harmonics and resonances so that a tiny input can lead to a very large effect. A group of men walking in step across a bridge can set up a rhythmic harmony that can destroy the bridge. A small rhythm in our lives, such as spending five minutes in silence every morning before leaping into action, can have a disproportionately large effect in ordering our lives and bringing greater balance and serenity into them. The more we can have a rhythm in our lives, especially one that is grounded in physical action, the more powerful and resonant with our world our energy can be.

Limits

Physical reality is based on limits and boundaries.

Traditional approaches to manifestation often assure us that we can "have it all" because the universe is one of abundance, and there are no limits upon what can come to us.

The truth is that there are limits. We live in a finite universe whose individual parts are defined by boundaries. In such a universe, I cannot "have it all." The idea that I can have it all, that there should be no limits at all upon my desires and my acquisitions, is rooted in infantile longings and a desire for security and comfort. Although it sounds empowering, it is actually a disempowering notion because it sees us not as creators but as consumers and receivers. It focuses upon our wants and upon our neediness. The implication is that we are sponges in an infinite ocean, surrounded by all the water we want and able to soak it up to our hearts' content. However, even a sponge eventually reaches saturation.

Everything manifests through taking on limits. That new car you may desire is not a smear of quantum possibilities; it is a specific particular automobile different and discernible from every other automobile. It is blue, not red or yellow. It has four doors, not two. It has six cylinders, not four, and so on. It has specific characteristics, each of which is a limit upon the full range of possible characteristics. Without those limits, it would not exist.

There is an important distinction here. To acknowledge limits is not the same as acknowledging limitation. Rather it is honoring those boundaries that make specificity possible. Limits permit diversity to exist. Limits make me different from you, and in that difference, creativity is possible between us.

Also the reality of the ecological age is that we need to act in recognition of the finite limits of our world system. We cannot act as if those limits did not exist. We cannot manifest an infinite world within a finite planet, with infinite numbers of people buying and consuming infinite numbers of goods and services. We cannot embrace a philosophy of limitlessness that has no sense of enough or of the boundaries that make distinctness and thus the power of focus possible.

Manifestation is the practice of a creative spirit, not of indulging unlimited desire. It is the practice of being a source, not a sponge. An appropriate understanding and acceptance of limits is what makes the difference.

The Moment

The power to manifest exists in the present moment, not in the past or in the future. The adage "Be here now" is good advice for successful manifestation. Dwelling inappropriately in the past or in the future traps vitality and attention. Giving mindful and loving attention to exactly what you are doing in this moment frees this energy, brings your passion into your current activity—no matter how dull or unlikable—and unleashes new transformative energies. If you do not like your present moment, now is the only time you can act to change it; you can't do anything about it yesterday or tomorrow. You live and act only in today.

Of course, planning for the future and enjoying or gaining wisdom from memories are important activities. There is a difference, however, between planning for a goal and worrying about the future, or between accessing memories for a purpose and constantly recapitulating old hurts or old glories. In one case your planning or your remembering serves an action in the present; in the other, you are abandoning the present with its potential for healing and change to live in a place that no longer exists or may never exist.

Though it can be a struggle at times, bringing your attention back to the present moment and being mindful of what you are doing, where you are, and whom you are with pays amazing dividends of increased energy and creativity. In effect, you are pulling your otherwise scattered consciousness away from past and future selves to attentiveness to your present self. You are fully inhabiting the moment. This puts you in touch with your full creative presence, not a partial self represented by memory or a potential self represented by your speculations about the future.

One way to pull your attentiveness to the present is to focus on learning. Is there anything novel that you can do or say to bring new energy or insight into the present situation? Is there anything you can learn about your self or the situation, about others or about your world, through mindful attention in the moment?

An attitude of openness to learning is a powerful tool for generating energy. We have all experienced those "aha!" moments when some new insight has broken through into our consciousness. Those moments are filled with energy and potential; in them, we are transformed. True learning, which brings new insights and understanding (as contrasted with the rote memorization of information), is a powerful form of incarnational manifestation. It brings a new you into being. It makes you comfortable with change and unfoldment. Every day I try to learn something new that will broaden my understanding of my self and my world. It is to my mind what exercise is to my body: a way of keeping supple and vital energy available in the present moment.

Practice mindfulness. Be conscious of what you are doing, no matter how repetitive or familiar it seems to you. The tendency is to drift off in our minds. Pay attention. Energy flows when you are mindfully connected to what you are doing and the environment in which you are doing it.

Forgiveness

One of the reasons we all find it difficult to live in the moment is that we focus upon the wounds we have suffered in the past. Those wounds, whether physical, emotional, mental, or financial, have become part of our identities. It is often safer to endure them—to suffer the memory of them—than to let them go and risk the changes that surely will follow. To surrender our woundedness is to go through a death and a rebirth, letting one identity fall away and another be born. That can be frightening, especially if we are not sure who the new person we become will be like.

Yet much of our creative energy can be bound up in reliving old wounds. We are called into the past by memories of hurts and betrayals and the desire for wrongs to be righted. We rehearse them; we play out scenarios of revenge and restitution. We ask for healing. But we are not healed because we don't really wish to be. To lose our wounds is to risk losing ourselves as we have come to know ourselves.

To liberate this energy bound into our past, the best solution I know is loving forgiveness for the wrongs and hurts we have suffered. Forgiveness is not admitting that our wounding was all right or that justice should not be done. It is forgoing the images of our pain in the light of a greater unity so that our energy can return to us in the present. It is giving ourselves permission to move forward and to be whole.

Forgiveness is never easy, because it means becoming reborn. In fact, you can make forgiveness of old wounds a manifestation project in its own right: manifesting a new you that is free from wounds.

Reclaiming your energy from your past is an important element in your manifestation fitness program; forgiveness may be the key tool in doing this. (For those who would like further information on forgiveness, please see the Bibliography.)

Wonderment

Another source of energy in the moment is a sense of wonderment and reverence toward life and toward the world around you. Wonderment is not wide-eyed naïveté; rather, it is an appreciation that there is mystery and miraculousness in life. Wonderment reminds us that there is much we don't know about the world we live in, including the miracle of life itself. It opens us to learning. Wonderment lets us see the world with fresh eyes that are alert to novelty and the presence of spirit. In this sense, it is like the "beginner's mind" that is spoken of in Zen practice.

Again, one way to achieve wonderment is to focus on the present. We never relive the same moment twice, but it requires attention to see the difference between this moment and all the preceding ones that seem just like it. At some time, everything we see about us now we saw for the first time. At that time, the world grabbed our attention. It allured us with its newness and drew us into itself. Our minds did not wander. They were captivated by what they were experiencing. Then familiarity set in. Like a film, it covered the windows of the soul, so that we saw with increasing dimness and then not at all. Instead we learned to see what we expected to see, what we had always seen; we saw our own projections.

To clean that film away, you must gaze again upon the world around you with a fierce attention. You must look fully, not partially, with part of you split off somewhere else. You must not be deceived by familiarity into thinking you need not be wholly present.

To cultivate this fresh seeing, go places or do things that are new for you. Recover the sense of wonderment, then keep it as part of your perception when you look at the things with which you are familiar. You will discover that even the most well-known person or place can hold surprises.

Another way to cultivate wonder is to pay attention to coincidences and synchronicities as they occur to us or to others around us. These are little miracles, as I have said, and are indicative of a wonderful mystery at work in creation. Acknowledge and appreciate them when they happen.

With wonderment comes a reverence for all existence. Honoring and delighting in the awesomeness of the cosmos around us as well as the life within us gives added power to the inner art of manifestation.

Possibility

An attitude closely aligned with that of wonderment is the sense of possibility. Possibility thinking is often taught as part of the techniques of manifestation and with good reason. It is very hard to imagine yourself manifesting a new job or a new relationship if you don't believe such a thing is possible. You do not have to know how something will happen, only that it is possible.

One key to possibility thinking is not to automatically say no to something. If you find yourself coming up with reasons why something can't happen before you've even thought the matter through, stop. You may not be able to think of any reason why it *could* happen, but at least stop denying the possibility. Give yourself a chance to consider alternatives before deciding that something can't be done.

Possibility thinking is not the same as saying that all things are possible. At any specific moment, not all things *are* possible. But possibility thinking avoids the automatic response that something is impossible simply because it has not happened before or it is unfamiliar or untried. Possibility thinking keeps you open to change and potential.

It has been my experience that many people draw the line of possibility too narrowly. The range of what they consider to be impossible is too broad. They may do this out of fear, out of a sense of unworthiness, out of laziness or even arrogance. ("If I can't do it, it can't be done!") Whatever the reason, they end up constraining their lives too much. A person may fail to try out for a job she wants because she feels she would never get it anyhow. The fact is, she won't know until she tries, but she won't try because she fears rejection and failure.

Possibility thinking entails an acceptance of risk. Mostly, though, it represents a broadening of your personal horizons, a spirit of adventure, and a willingness to suspend automatic judgment.

Positive Being

The idea of positive thinking is central to most teachings on manifestation. However, for me what is more important is a larger quality I call positive being.

Teachings on positive thinking generally concentrate on eliminating negative thoughts, the doubts, fears, and questions that might interfere with accomplishing a goal. However, in the right context, doubts, fears, and questioning can lead to important insights. They represent a person's struggle to go deeper into his own soul and into the soul of the world. Going into our fears and doubts, listening to them and learning from them, can bring us to a new awareness and a deeper attunement with the holistic power of life.

We need a broader and more systemic way of measuring positivity than simply looking to see if our thoughts are always good and encouraging and our feelings always up and bouncy. Our true powerful positivity is made up of more than just a succession of positive affirmations and thoughts. It arises from the health and balance of our whole lives, which includes the darker elements as well as the lighter ones. Sometimes doubt, anger, fear, depression, or despair signal the movement of deep transformative forces within the psyche; they are signs of inner transformations and psychic shifts. Or they reflect genuine problems and imbalances in our social and natural environment. In either case, to push such feelings and thoughts away or to deny them in the interests of a surface positivity is to bind our energy, not to liberate it.

It is the energy from your whole life—the energy of your presence—that will ultimately support and vitalize your acts of manifestation. The occasional doubt or fear, worry or negative thought will not disrupt the process.

Gratitude

Recognizing and appreciating the blessings in your life—indeed, the fact of your life itself—is an attitude that also opens you to the larger flow of creative and spiritual energy in the world. Being grateful allows you to see all that is done for you by others; it is a corrective to a selfish and victimized point of view. You begin to see how much that is truly important in your life is actually a gift. A relationship that is coerced or that is dealt with as a transaction is never as powerful nor as rewarding as one in which all concerned willingly give of themselves. Being grateful makes you more open to giving more freely yourself, which attunes you to the flow of love within creation. In its ability to energize and liberate your life, gratitude has no equal. Being grateful for all you have received and for what you will (or hope to) receive, as well as being grateful for your opportunities to give in return, is without parallel for empowering the process of the inner art.

Spirituality

Gratefulness is a natural component of a spiritual practice. Other components are important, too, in expanding the potentiality and energy of your current reality.

A spiritual path can take many forms. It can be very simple or very complex. Dr. William Bloom, in his excellent introductory book on spirituality, *First Steps*, lists three basic components of a spiritual practice: daily alignment with the sacred, however you may understand that term; daily self-reflection, particularly as to motives and intents behind your actions; and some way of daily embodying your spirituality in action and attitudes, as, for example, through service or in the way you relate to people.

In my own teaching, I use almost an identical schema. However you interpret and engage with a spiritual path, though, its value in manifestation lies not in any particular dogma, belief system, or cosmology; it lies in learning to interact with transpersonal perspectives and energies. It lies in learning a discipline of transcending the self, while also loving the self in new and deeper ways. It lies in learning compassion and a sense of our interconnectedness within the beingness of the sacred. It lies in experiencing the communion of spirit at the heart of the cosmos.

The inner art is, after all, an *inner* art. By its very nature, it engages us with a spiritual dimension. To have other ways of encountering that dimension and making it part of our lives, particularly in ways that are aligned with experiences of wholeness, can only help the inner art reach its full potential.

Compassionate Engagement

With the exception of forgiveness, all the manifestation fitness exercises I have suggested so far have been self-oriented. They are things you do in yourself or for yourself.

What helps keep your current reality vital and attuned to larger possibilities is for it not to be entirely self-referencing. Some people collapse into themselves and their constricted view of reality and possibility like a star collapsing into a black hole. Reaching out to others, giving of yourself, engaging with points of view and ways of being different from your own, being of service, staying connected and involved are all ways of preventing this.

Here are some suggested fitness exercises for engaging compassionately with your world.

Generosity

Being grateful for what others have done for you can inspire you to pass on the favor. Almost all manifestation eventually comes to you through a human channel, that is, through the actions of another person; you can be such a channel yourself.

The paradox of manifestation is that while it seems to be an art of getting things, it actually is enabled by what you give away. It is powered by love and generosity.

Nothing expands your reality and connects it with higher potentials of energy more fully than being a source yourself of energy, joy, possibilities, and help for others.

When I have meditated upon the art of manifestation, I often touch into a spiritual domain where the dominant quality is a spirit of abundance. This spirit, I believe, is one of the fundamental creative forces in the universe. In the cosmic drive toward complexity and emergence, diversity and abundance appear to be universal attributes. You need only look at the rich variety of life-forms here on earth to see this.

Part of the art of manifestation is to embody abundance.

Abundance is a loaded term. It is often used to mean having everything we want and need and more besides. There is an implication of surplus and of unending supply.

From my experience with the inner art, I do not define abundance as a quantitative state but rather as a qualitative one. Abundance is the presence of possibility and openness to emergence. It is a willingness to give in order that something else can come into being.

Some of the richest and most abundant people I know actually possess very little but move through their days in an aura of creative potential. Life seems more vital around them and achieving new possibilities seems less difficult or obstructed when you are with them. They are inspiring simply through their presence.

WEALTH

Related to abundance is the idea of being a creator of wealth in which all may share.

Wealth, like *abundance*, is one of those loaded terms. It can mean money or other financial or tangible assets. Lately, information is being seen as a form of wealth.

In this context, though, I think of wealth not as an asset that you own but as a condition that empowers. It nourishes that which is and makes possible the emergence of that which could be.

Wealth-creating is inherent in the universe. Since it first exploded into being in the Big Bang, the cosmos has been creating wealth. It has evolved from very simple atomic structures to create galaxies, stars, life-forms, and ideas, and galaxies, stars, life-forms, and ideas all give birth to yet more life, more possibility, more forms within the universe.

I see wealth and abundance as emerging from the convergence of diversity, interconnectedness, and co-creativity. When these three work together, there is a blending of differences and an enlargement of possibility and accomplishment. When they are denied, there is scarcity.

If I think of wealth as something to own and accumulate just for myself, especially at the expense of someone else, I break the power of this convergence. By impoverishing another, I ultimately impoverish myself. I certainly deny to my reality the energy and vitality that come out of the domains of connectedness and wholeness. Wealth is ultimately a co-created phenomenon. The more I can be someone who embodies wealth by nourishing and assisting the well-being, development, and creativity of others, the more my wealth will increase and the more powerful will be the energy that is available to my manifestations.

Consider the ways in which you are wealthy and how that wealth can be used to enhance your world.

UNOBSTRUCTEDNESS
Sometimes, though, the way we empower, manifest, create wealth, and increase abundance in our world is by doing nothing more than getting out of the way. It is the practice of unobstructedness, of standing aside and letting life get on with helping someone else.

Here is a wonderful story about that with which I close this chapter.

Caroline Myss is an outstanding medical intuitive and clairvoyant, as well as a writer and teacher. Consequently, she is much in demand as a consultant by doctors and as a speaker by groups. Being a consummate professional, once she agrees to an engagement, she will move heaven and earth to fulfill her commitment.

She was scheduled to give a lecture at a conference in Denver but became ill with a nasty virus only a few days before. In her usual pattern, she would have gone and toughed it out. But this time, something in her said she should not go but help the conference organizers find a substitute.

She ended up recommending another woman who was a doctor and teacher whose work specialized in the convergence of spirituality and medicine. With only a day or so to make the substitution, the conference organizers called the doctor's office only to be told that she was away on a trip, but that she would be in Denver on the weekend where she was giving a lecture in the same hotel where they were holding their conference.

On Saturday, the conference organizers discovered that the doctor was lecturing in a room directly across the hall from the room in which their program was going on! Hoping it wasn't too late, they walked across the hall and talked to the doctor, and she graciously agreed to fill in for Caroline. Her impromptu talk at their conference later that day was a great success. Afterward, she was approached by an editor who had been in the audience. He said he had been wanting to meet her and that he was most excited about what she had said in her lecture. Would she be willing to write a book for him? The doctor was ecstatic, and before the day was finished, she had a book contract in her hands.

Sometimes, as in Caroline's case in this story, you are only the means for someone else's manifestation to occur. Being sensitive to when that is so is definitely part of your manifestation fitness program. It can only enhance the vitality of your reality.

Chapter Six

Your Manifestation Project

Starting a manifestation project is a bit like starting a garden: It is an activity of nourishing and growing something rather than just attracting it. If I want carrots in my garden, I do not attract them; I grow them from carrot seeds. The inner art is analogous to this. We grow what we wish from within ourselves.

This gardening process proceeds in three stages. The first is to assess the nature of that which you wish to manifest and its connectedness with you. That is what this chapter is about.

The second stage is to create a seed image, which you will plant in the soil of your own being. That is the subject of the next chapter.

The third stage is to grow that seed by connecting it with nourishing energy from within yourself and from the world at large. That we will cover in Chapters 7 and 8.

Assessing Your Project

When you embark on a manifestation project, you probably have in mind just what it is you want. It may be an object, a person, or a condition, such as a new job or better health. It can also be an inner state, such as greater clarity about some issue or peace of mind. Chances are you are thinking about the form of what you want: what it looks like, what it will do, how it will function, and so forth. To a greater or lesser degree, you can visualize the form of what you are seeking to manifest.

Your first task, once you know what it is you want, is to form some basic conclusions about the relationship you have with your objective at the beginning of your manifestation project. This is a preliminary attunement with the project itself. What is the nature of your manifestation? How will you know when it succeeds?

You are going to do this by answering a series of questions. Please write down your answers; it helps to ground what you are doing. If you wish, you can even imagine that which you wish to manifest appearing before you and asking it the questions while you are in a meditative or quiet state. If you do the latter, write down any answers, impressions, images, sensations, or feelings that come to you.

The purpose of this exercise is to clarify just what kind of energy exists between you and your objective at the outset. Think of it as a project assessment exercise to see how much energy there really is in it for you. If, when you have completed it, you find that you really don't have that much energy going between you and your objective, then chances are you may have been responding to an impulse or perhaps a suggestion from someone else. (Advertisements are a good source of such suggestions!) You then don't need to proceed any further.

On the other hand, if this project is still compelling to you, then you can proceed to the next step, which involves deeper inner work to create the seed image of your manifestation.

Adapting the Process

One note before we proceed. The following questions plus the exercises in the next chapter are designed to illustrate a process as much as to provide specific steps. Not every question may be appropriate to your specific manifestation objective; likewise, you may need to tailor the exercises in the next chapter to fit your needs. What is important is that you understand the reasons behind the questions and the exercises so that you can adapt them as necessary.

Manifesting Money

This is particularly true if what you wish to manifest is money. In the context of the inner art, money is an abstraction. It represents a means to an end, not necessarily the end in itself. I have found few people who wish to manifest money for its own sake; usually the money is needed for some other purpose, such as paying a debt or funding a project. Money may be received as a way of fulfilling your manifestation, but making money the actual object of your manifestation project creates some special challenges.

In working the inner art, you are dealing not only with the forms of things but with their inner dimensions as well. You are weaving a new energy of reality around the form, pattern, essence, and unity of your objective. But what is the form of $250 or $5,000 or any other sum you may wish to manifest? What is its pattern or its essence? Do you visualize a pile of cash or a bank statement showing you have received the desired amount? You *can* do this, but the whole process I teach will work more effectively if instead of a sum of money, you make as your objective the specific item, condition, or relationship for which you want the money.

On the other hand, once you have created a seed image for your manifestation project—an image built around an object, condition, or person—then you can use a sum of money as a symbol to represent that image.

For example, you may wish to manifest $3,000 to pay a debt. Instead of using the money itself as the object, visualize the condition of being free from debt. Imagine what that will feel like in all the areas of your life. For example, what effect would that freedom have in how your body feels (less stress?), to your relationships (more openness, more energy?), and to your spirit (greater inner peace?). It is that effect you wish to manifest. Use it as your objective.

Paradoxically, the very specificity of a sum of money can limit your manifestation, since it doesn't allow much room for alternatives. In the above example, by making ending the indebtedness your objective rather than a particular amount of money, you leave open the door that the debt might be canceled through another means. For example, if you are indebted to a person, that person might be moved to turn the money into a gift. (If you owe the money to a bank, though, you might as well continue to focus on the exact sum! The bank is.)

Attuning Through Questions

If you understand that you may need to adapt the following process to match your unique manifestation project, let us proceed with the questions.

WHY DO I WISH TO MANIFEST THIS?

To be successful, you need to be clear about why you wish to undertake your manifestation project. Sometimes the reason seems pretty obvious ("I want a new job because my old one has ended, and I need work"). The surface motivation *is* all there is to it (although even here, some deeper exploration may reveal unexpected dividends).

On the other hand, the surface motivation or desire may mask more important issues. Tapping into those issues may release a clearer and more creative energy to fuel the manifestation process. This is especially so if you discover that underneath the personal motivation is something that ties you into the collective well-being. You may, for example, want a particular job for the money and security it offers or because the work interests you, and then discover when you probe more deeply that what really attracts you is an idealistic response, feeling that the job (or the money it brings you) would give you greater opportunities for service to your community. Aligning your manifestation with this motivation for service allows you to tap more fully the sources of energy arising from more inclusive and spiritual levels of connectedness.

The reverse is also true: You may tell yourself that you want something for noble and altruistic reasons, when your real motivation is simple self-interest or greed. ("If I get that high-paying job, I will be able to give more to charity; of course, I'll also have my mansion, my BMW, and my yacht!") This deception can limit the overall energy to which you have access.

Manifesting something purely for self-interest is not wrong in itself. It is when we pretend to ourselves and others that we are doing otherwise that we set up inner patterns of deception. If we do so frequently and habitually, then we damage inner foundations of alignment and trust that help sustain a clear and positive energy in our lives upon which the process of manifestation can draw.

What is my natural connection with my manifestation?

Natural connections or affinities can act to empower the manifestation. The connections could be through environment (the person with whom you wish to manifest a relationship works in your office, for example), interest, other relationships, and so forth. The connections may be through your passion and the flow of your life.

For example, I like computers and use them in different ways in my work; I also like the idea of boating, but I have rarely sailed, and I am not always comfortable away from dry land. It would be fun to go sailing, but I don't think of it much, while I quite often think about new computer systems and upgrading the one that I own. Manifesting a computer falls more easily within the flow of my passion than does manifesting a boat, which is more a passing interest. I have a natural connection with computers that is not there with boats.

The fact that there may be little or no natural connection between you and that which you wish to manifest does not mean the manifestation is not possible, only that there is no natural flow of interest and excitement between you to energize the process. Consequently, you must be more mindful and deliberate in directing energy toward your desire.

What natural congruency exists between us?

Congruency is a measure of how harmonious that which you wish to manifest is with your present reality. How well or how easily do the two fit together? It may be something you desire, but does it really blend into your life and pattern? If it does not, then what changes need to take place to make the connection more harmonious?

Congruency can deal with any aspect or level of your life. A manifestation can be congruent or incongruent with your financial condition. (It is not congruent, for example, to manifest a $1,000 stereo system when you cannot otherwise pay your rent or feed your family; on the other hand, if you are a professional musician and you need the sound system for your work to bring in an income, that is another matter altogether.) It can be congruent or incongruent with your professional status, with your talents, your skills, your environment, your current relationships, and so forth. When dealing with individuals or with conditions involving individuals, congruency includes harmony of wills. You may wish to manifest me, but if I do not wish to be manifested by you, then we are not congruent in our purposes. We may have a physical affinity but little in common emotionally or mentally, or we may have congruency of wills and purpose and be incongruent in our professions, where we live, or our priorities in life.

Depending on the nature and extent of the incongruity, you may have difficulty seeing your manifestation as a potential reality. If that which you wish to manifest seems very incongruent with your current reality, it probably will not seem real to you; then the manifestation process will be much more difficult.

HOW COMPATIBLE IS THAT WHICH I WISH TO MANIFEST WITH MY WHOLENESS?

Is it compatible with your body's health, your psychological well-being, your spiritual alignment, your relationships, and your capacity as a creative and productive person? Does it diminish or enhance your inner presence?

Many things you may try to manifest may be neutral in this regard. (Manifesting a toaster is probably not going to affect your communion with God.) But if compatibility is an issue, it can be a very important one that blocks your attunement to your manifestation project. Likewise, a manifestation might be congruent in the sense that it has a strong potential for becoming real in your life and still be incompatible with you in some way.

For example, I may be committed to fostering ecological balance and avoiding pollution. Manifesting a car may be congruent with the facts of my reality but incongruent with my values. I can see many possible ways in which I could manifest a car, but to do so would be incompatible with my desire to live lightly on the earth, not burn fossil fuels, not pollute, and so forth. If for some reason I need to manifest a car, then I must deal with the impact and influence of my values upon the manifestation process itself. I have congruity but not compatibility.

Many values exist at an intellectual or feeling level, but manifestation involves other levels as well. The issue of compatibility needs to be explored at the levels of pattern, essence, and unity, as well as at the levels of form and content. So ask yourself how compatible your manifestation is (or will be when successful) with your alignment and relationship with your own deeper self and with the sacred. How might it affect the wholeness and harmony of your being—your essence—and the spiritual attunement that aligns you with a sense of unity? How compatible is this manifestation with the well-being of those around you who are part of your pattern? Who might be hurt or helped by this manifestation?

Looking at this collective side to your manifestation will enable you to pinpoint possible allies or opponents, as well as possible consequences; it enables you to be ethically or morally discerning about whether to proceed with the manifestation.

AM I WILLING TO ACCEPT WHATEVER CHANGE
THE MANIFESTATION WILL BRING ABOUT? WHAT
CHANGES MIGHT THESE BE?

Every successful manifestation (and perhaps even some un-successful ones) will bring about change. At the very least you are going from the person who does not have what you want to the person who does. Plus what you manifest will bring with it patterns and consequences that require you to change in some way.

A lack of connection, incongruity, or incompatibility can all be lessened by a willingness to change. To return to my earlier example, as someone concerned about pollution and the environment, I may have to change my unwillingness to participate in the automotive-petroleum industry by virtue of owning a car if I want to manifest one for transportation.

As much as possible, whatever change you make should be knowing and mindful. You may well not be able to anticipate every little change that a successful manifestation could bring about, so the issue becomes one of identifying those changes that are obvious. It is also a matter of willingness to change because of the manifestation. If you want something but you are not willing to accept the changes it might bring, then you will withhold part of your presence from the manifestation process, which can block its success. For example, a person may say he or she is trying to manifest a spouse, but if that person does not wish to give up the freedom of being single, then that unwillingness to change is a block to the manifestation. Remember, manifestation is not a process of control and manipulation using some magical means. When you manifest, you are a participant in a relationship in which you also are vulnerable and subject to transformation.

To the best of your knowledge, what changes are inherent in your manifestation? How willing are you to make those changes?

What contribution will I make to that which I wish to manifest?

How will you receive whatever it is you are manifesting into your life in a way that makes it better than it was—more enriched in its own incarnation than it was before? How will you add to its purposes and intentions?

Of course, what you contribute to a toaster or a car is different from what you would contribute to a person, a relationship, or a job. However, manifestation is a two-way street. What are you willing to commit or to do for the well-being of that which you are manifesting?

It is easy to know what you wish your manifestation to do for you. You've already explored that as part of the desire or need you feel for that object, person, or condition. It requires a flip of perception to attune to what you can do for your manifestation. Yet the more you can be aware of what you will give or do, both to make the manifestation possible and to honor it after it has succeeded, the richer and more co-creative will be the energy you have flowing through your manifestation project.

Answering these six questions will give you deeper insight into the nature of your manifestation. It is possible upon reflection that you may decide to cancel or change your manifestation project because of the insights you have gained. On the other hand, the fact that there are incongruities or a lack of natural connections, for example, does not mean that your manifestation cannot succeed; it only means that these factors and their possible consequences need to be taken into account.

ON A SCALE OF ONE TO TEN, HOW MUCH DO I
REALLY WANT OR NEED THIS MANIFESTATION?
HOW DEEP DOES THIS DESIRE GO? WHAT IS
THE EXTENT OF MY COMMITMENT TO THIS
MANIFESTATION PROJECT?

You need to know just how much energy and passion is
present in this manifestation for you. The strength of your desire or need is one of the sources that fuels the process, both
because desire generates a field of energy in its own right and
because it measures how willing you will be to stick with your
manifestation project and continue to nourish it. It is a measure
of your commitment to do the inner work (and possibly outer
work as well) necessary to complete the process.

You also want to know just where this desire comes from. We
are all moved daily by surface desires that arise like waves on a
lake before a breeze, only to disappear just as quickly. With
advertisements on television, radio, newspapers, magazines,
buses, billboards, and even the sides of buildings, we live in an
environment calculated to inspire desire. We can be stimulated
into wanting something or feeling we need something, but that
feeling is not really very deep. It survives until the next wave
comes along. It has taken on the energy of excitement generated by the advertisement, but that energy does not connect
very deeply with you or engage your deeper passion and interest. You soon lose it.

So what has stimulated your desire for you? Is it a need? Is it
something arising from within you? Or is it a projection from
your environment? If it is the latter, it may not have the "juice"
necessary to sustain your manifestation project.

This is not to say that an impulsive desire cannot be the
focus of or bring about a manifestation, because it can if conditions are right and your own general attunement with your
world is good and energetic. It is just that you want to honor
the craft, the inner art, with which you intend to work.

Think of it like an artist. Creating a sculpture, painting a painting, or writing a poem requires commitment to see the project through its necessary steps to completion. If you are always starting but never finishing, you will build a habit that dissipates your energy and acts as an obstacle to becoming proficient in your craft. You will never enter the depths of your art if you keep bouncing off its surface.

Manifestation is also a craft. It needs to be honored with your time and commitment and your willingness to see it through to the end. You won't touch the deeper levels of this art unless you do.

Are there other alternatives that would satisfy this desire?

You know what you want, but are there other ways of achieving that objective? If you are seeking to manifest a particular job, would a different kind of job do just as well? Are you manifesting a specific house or simply a new place to live? How much leeway is there in how your manifestation can unfold and the form it can take?

What other avenues might there be to manifesting what I wish?

Not everything need be attained using a manifestation project. There may be other methods available to you that are more direct and appropriate. If you can just buy what you want, or earn it, or save for it, you do not need a manifestation project to do so.

I may say, for example, "I want to manifest a new computer system." The thought behind this statement is, "I don't have the money right now to upgrade my computer, but when I do, I will do so." Do I really need to create a manifestation project for this? It's not that I don't know how to get my new computer. I can begin saving my money for it and perhaps look for ways of increasing my income. Thinking that I might manifest it in a magical way may, in fact, make me neglect what I need to do practically to bring my desire about.

On the other hand, practicing the art of manifestation connects us with the deeper forces in our lives, and that is a good thing. I can set up a manifestation project even for something I know I can buy or acquire in normal ways because I want the experience of entering into this action from as holistic a place as I can reach within myself. I want my acquisition to be harmonious with me, in tune with my wholeness, and a product of conscious co-creation. I am using the project, then, as a practice in attunement rather than specifically as a means of getting something.

Making an End Statement

Finally, after you have gone through these questions (and any others you might think of to help you evaluate and assess your project), and after you have decided to go ahead, there is one other thing to do. Write out as specifically as you can just how you will know when your manifestation project has ended. You may not know how you will receive whatever it is you are manifesting, but you have some idea now what the final result will be. Write down how your project will end.

We all manifest every day in an open-ended way. We are generating a co-creative field that aligns and shapes reality as much as it can to coincide with the character of our holistic identity. We never know just when a coincidence, a synchronicity, a lucky break, or a miracle will appear in our lives, but we are always in touch with the basic organizing, generative, creative force in the universe that allows such things to happen without our consciously having to think about them.

A manifestation project is different. It has a beginning and an ending. It has a clear goal you are seeking to achieve. To aid in this process, you need to formulate this goal as clearly and specifically as you can. This is your statement of purpose. Like writing a business plan or a request for a loan from a bank, writing it out helps to take your manifestation out of the abstract and down into the concrete, which is where you want it to take place anyway. It enables you to clearly see that you are manifesting something specific and particular; you are transforming energy from the realm of the wave to the realm of the particle.

Incubation

When you have done all this, put your answers to your questions and your end statement away for three days. During that time, don't look at them or think about your manifestation project. Let the energy you invoked in this process so far incubate.

After three days have passed, take out your file. Read over the questions and the answers and see how you respond to them now. Do you have any further insights? If so, write them down. Are you still interested? Is the project still exciting for you? Are all systems go?

A Journal

If so, then create a journal. In it you will keep various items about your project. Here you will write down and keep not only the exercises you will do and their results but any other thoughts, images, ideas, dreams, insights, attunements, coincidences, synchronicities, and so forth that arise as you proceed. Use this journal to keep a record of your project and your progress in using the inner art. Also it can be a place for any other reflections and insights that come to you as a result of your attunement to your own deeper levels.

With your journal ready, it is time to proceed to the inner work, creating the seed image that you will work with. I call this the genetics of manifestation.

Chapter Seven

The Genetics of
Manifestation

In 1962, James Watson and Francis Crick received the Nobel prize for their work in determining the molecular structure of DNA. It was they who first proposed the image of the double helix, strands of nucleotides twining about each other in a spiral of identity, joined by bonds of hydrogen atoms.

This was also the year I entered Arizona State University. I already knew that I was interested in a career in science, but in which science? The image of the double helix inspired me. I was drawn by the elegance and beauty of the concept. The result was that I determined to be a molecular biologist and make genetics the area of my specialty. I probably had visions of my own Nobel prize one day!

Of course, as I have already related, my life took a different turn of its own, for if science was one of the spirals in my own double helix, spirituality and an awareness of inner dimensions was the other. In the end, it was the latter that proved dominant and turned me into a free-lance mystic with an interest in science, rather than a scientist with an interest in mysticism. (I'm not sure who lost and who gained in that process, the scientists or the mystics!)

Still, the image of the double helix remains a powerful one for me; so, not surprisingly, I use it as a metaphor for the next step in your manifestation project. This is creating the spiraling interaction of resonance and attunement—the double helix—between you and that which you wish to manifest that will be the "DNA" of the body of your manifestation.

Imagine the DNA molecule. You have probably seen pictures of the two strands twisting and curving about each other. Each strand contains four nitrogenous bases: adenine, guanine, thymine, and cytosine. (Don't worry; the names are not pertinent to manifestation, but indulging my background, it was fun to throw in some scientific jargon!) It is at these four bases that the two strands are joined by bonds of hydrogen, a bonding that unites the strands and forms the double helix.

With this image in mind as a metaphor, consider yourself and the object of your desire. You are each strands of identity, strands of being, curving from the most particulate level of material existence to the wavelike levels of the enfolded order, unity, and the mystery of the sacred. Like chemical DNA, you seek to connect at four points: as forms, as patterns, as essences, and as participants in unity.

When you have those four connections firmly in mind and a felt sense of what they create together, you have crafted the metaphysical, manifestational DNA of your objective, something that is neither just you nor just your objective but the co-incarnational, co-creative blend of both. You have the inner double helix that you will nourish as it unfolds to become the substance of your manifestation.

In practical terms, this double helix will take the form of a psychological and spiritual construct or image. This is more than just a visual image of what you are seeking to manifest, because it contains information not only about the form of the manifestation but also about its connections and relationships, its soul, and its oneness with unity. For simplicity's sake, though, I call this construct the seed image.

Creating a Seed Image

Every form of manifestation of which I am aware involves some kind of visualization. Usually, what you are visualizing is the form of your objective. Remember the story of my friend at Findhorn who was seeking to manifest a guitar and surrounded himself with pictures of the kind of guitar he wanted to help him visualize it?

In my approach, this kind of surface visualization is a starting point, but you need to go deeper. You need to visualize what is behind the surface, inside the shape, beneath the appearances. I call this deep visualization. Using it, you look at the form, pattern, essence, and unity of that which you wish to manifest. It is this process that you will use to create your seed image, for it is this seed image that you wish to visualize and energize as part of your manifestation project.

To begin with, pick some object, condition, or relationship with a person that you would like to manifest. Then follow along as I describe the process, using selected exercises to illustrate it. Please note that at the end of each exercise, you should write down in your manifestation project journal any images, feelings, insights, intuitions, or the like that may come to you as a result.

Doing the Exercises

To do the exercises in this book, begin just by sitting down and letting yourself relax. Sink into a feeling of stillness and calm. Take some deep calming breaths, then simply watch your breathing. Don't try to breathe in a particular way. Close your eyes. Perhaps you can imagine a scene that is peaceful and calming to you. Thoughts may come, but just observe them without judgment and let them go. If you find yourself becoming distracted, simply return to watching your breathing. Let yourself continue to relax, but do not fall asleep. Imagine yourself as a hunter watching a game trail. You want to be still so as not to scare away the wild animals, but you want to be poised and alert as well. With a little practice, this state of alert calmness or poised stillness will begin to come more easily to you.

When you are asked to visualize, simply close your eyes and imagine a television or movie screen on the inside of your eyelids. Using your imagination, see the scene you wish or the one being described to you in the exercises as if it were being projected onto that screen.

If at any time in any exercise or visualization you begin to feel uncomfortable or the experience is too intense in some way, simply open your eyes and reestablish contact with your normal reality. Take a couple of deep breaths. Get up and move about, perform some familiar task, or get something to eat and drink to "ground" your energy. Any discomfort will quickly pass. You are certainly in no danger, and you are always in control.

Also, remember, as I mentioned in the last chapter, these exercises are suggestions and illustrations. If you can think of different ways that may be more natural to you or more appropriate to what you are manifesting to accomplish the same conditions of attunement, then feel free to adapt. After all, what is important here is understanding the process, not following a preset recipe.

It would be a good idea to read through all the exercises first before trying to do any of them. This will give you a sense of the overall purpose and flow of what you are doing with them.

The Seed's Form

The following three exercises deal with visualizing the form of that which you intend to manifest, your own form, and how the two connect and blend. They are the first step in building the double helix of your seed image. Their purpose is to give you a sense of what the success in your manifestation would feel like as a physical reality.

❧

Exercise:
IMAGING THE FORM OF YOUR OBJECTIVE

This is the easiest part of deep visualization. Simply imagine what the object of your manifestation looks like. Use as many of your senses as are appropriate. That is, imagine what this form smells like, tastes like, sounds like, and feels like, as well as what it looks like. Visualize it in three dimensions from a variety of different angles or perspectives. The idea is to make the image as full-bodied and real as you can. If you have the skill for it, make a drawing that represents this form to you, or find pictures or symbols from magazines and other sources. Paste or tape them onto a sheet of paper or some other appropriate surface where you can see them and use them to assist your visualization.

In most manifestation techniques, clarity of image is extolled as a virtue. Certainly, it is harder to work with a fuzzy image than a clear one. Specificity can be a virtue. However, what is important is not necessarily the clarity of the image in itself but its clarity *to you*. Just what this means depends on what you are trying to manifest, but the objective is that it feels real to you.

While it is easy to imagine the form of an object or a person, it is more complex to imagine a condition like a new job or better relationships. If I want to manifest happiness or creativity or friendship, I need to decide just what those things mean to me. I need to come up with some specific concrete images of what I would be experiencing if I were happy or creative or had a friend. Simply saying "happiness" is far too vague and undefined to offer any focus or energy to the manifestation process.

When I am manifesting a condition, I may actually need to use a collage of images. No one image may quite capture for me what I want, so I may need to hold several images in mind at once or make up a composite image.

For example, Peter wants a specific kind of car; Susan, however, simply wants reliable transportation, which she assumes will be a car. Peter starts with a clear and detailed image of the car he wants, including its make and model, the year, the interior and exterior color, and specific options.

Susan's image, though, is not so detailed. She isn't concerned about the kind of car she can manifest; she just wants something that will get her where she needs to go and home again. In fact, as she forms her image and meditates on it, she realizes that what she really wants to manifest is not an object but a condition. Although a car would satisfy her need, other things might satisfy it as well. She might meet someone who invites her into a convenient carpool. She might move to a place where public transportation is readily available. She might get a bicycle. When she wants to make a special trip, she could rent a car. In other words, other options are available besides owning a car herself.

Susan is actually imaging what the condition of *having transportation* would mean to her. She needs to be as specific as possible about the ways this condition could be fulfilled in her life; part of this specificity could entail imagining specific feelings she would have if her transportation needs were met.

EXERCISE:
IMAGING YOUR FORM

Form a clear image of yourself as you begin this manifestation project. Feel into the nature of your own physical presence. Feel the reality that it gives to your life. In your body, you can truly be here now. Observe how your body locates you in the physical universe, how it anchors you in time and space. Appreciate the power latent in just the simple fact of being material in a world of other material objects and people. Your body is the gateway into the realm of substance.

This exercise should be even easier than the previous one. (If you have difficulty with it, sit in front of a mirror while you do it.) Basically, you are acknowledging that your physicality—

your body—is the lever that moves whatever exists in the realm of ideas, imagination, and spirit into the material world. All manifestation ultimately engages you physically. Whatever it is you wish to manifest, eventually you must deal with it as a physical person. It becomes part of your incarnation, part of the responsibility of your life.

In the inner art of manifestation, your body is a tremendous ally.

At some point, your physical form must intersect and engage with the physical form of your objective. Even if what you are seeking to manifest is an inner condition, it will have validity only if you can embody it. It must be real to the cells of your body, otherwise it is only a thought, a dream, a hope.

When you can feel the presence—the inner reality—of your manifestation in your body, you have made one of the four connections that wind your mutual strands of metaphysical DNA together. The double helix of the seed image is beginning to form.

Exercise:
Connecting the Forms

Imagine you and your manifestation objective together in a physical way. If you are manifesting a person, see yourself with that person, taking a walk, talking, riding in a car, eating dinner together, whatever seems appropriate. If you are manifesting an object, see that object in your possession. If you are manifesting an inner state, see yourself acting out of that state; for example, if you are manifesting confidence, see yourself in a situation in which you normally might be shy or unsure but in which you are now acting with confidence.

As you construct your scene, make it as real as you can using imagery that draws on your physical senses. See whatever there is to see, in color and with detail; hear whatever there is to hear, smell any odors that might naturally be part of that scene (you might be in a pine forest, for example, smelling the trees), and so forth.

Imagine that what you are doing is looking into an alternate reality, one that represents the fulfillment of your manifestation. Furthermore, you are imaging your manifestation in a tangible way as part of a physical reality.

When the scene is stable and clear to you, do not analyze it but appreciate it. Attune to it. Feel into its reality. Step into it and be in its reality for a time. In your scene, the fulfillment of your manifestation is real, and it is the quality of this reality that you want to experience within your body.

The object of this exercise is to make the physical connection with your objective real to your body awareness, so that its deep level of awareness can add its energy to affirming and manifesting this reality.

The Seed's Pattern

You do not exist in a vacuum, all by yourself. You are connected in a web of relationships with ancestors, family, friends, co-workers, places, possessions, activities, and so forth. In the co-incarnational view of the universe, all these people, places, conditions, and things are your co-incarnates.

We are generally not used to thinking of ourselves as embodied patterns, but we are. The pattern we inhabit might be thought of as our extended body, a "wide body" or energy field. We carry its invisible (and sometimes not so invisible) presence with us wherever we go, and its influence often becomes a lens through which we interact with our world. When two people meet, it is like two galaxies passing through each other or two spiderwebs dancing together in the breeze: patterns intersecting with patterns.

In the inner art of manifestation, the concept of pattern has a dual significance. In the first place, it is a locus of identity and energy within you that you can draw upon. In the second place, it is an aspect of that which you are manifesting that you need to consider. It allows you to see more deeply just what it is you are manifesting and how you may need to adjust your reality accordingly.

The seed image you are building right now in this process represents the new reality you wish to shift into focus, so to speak. Your ability to fully understand and image this new reality is limited unless you consider the implications of how you and your objective come together as patterns, galaxy to galaxy, web to web.

❧

EXERCISE:
IMAGING YOUR PATTERN

It is possible to explore your pattern as information, like a family tree that shows how all your ancestors and relatives are connected. However, for our purposes, what I want you to focus on is not the information of how you are connected but the nature of the energy that emerges from the fact that you are connected.

The following questions are suggestive of what you will be looking for in this exercise: Who are you as a co-incarnated being? What quality of energy do you bring into your life from the character of your interconnections? What is the nature and energy of the "you" who is the result, the co-creation, of all your connections?

Imagine yourself in a room surrounded by five mirrors. The lighting is such that you can see yourself in each mirror, but your face is shadowed. One mirror is labeled "Ancestors," one is labeled "Family," the third is labeled "Friends," and the fourth is labeled "Work." The last mirror is unlabeled.

Look into the Ancestral mirror. You see yourself as you are now, but as you watch, around and behind your reflection other images form. They are your ancestors. You can see images that represent your parents, your grandparents, and older generations as well; you may even see archetypal figures representing your racial and ethnic heritage.

These images surround your reflection, and as you watch, they begin to blur and to merge, forming an aura of light around your image. In this light, your image shifts in some manner; where before it was shadowed, now you can see yourself more clearly. What you see, though, is not you as you normally are but you as you emerge from your ancestral connections. It is you as you are co-created by your family's heritage.

Pay attention to this image. What do you look like? What kind of energy do you feel from this figure? What does it have to offer you? Does it say anything or do anything? Pay attention.

When you feel you are finished looking at your ancestral self, turn and look at your family self. This is you connected to your present family, your spouse, your children, your brothers and sisters, your cousins. If you have no current family, then this mirror is blank, or you can rename it to look at another area of connections in your life.

Repeat the process with this mirror, observing what reflection emerges as the co-incarnational product of your nonancestral familial relationships. Pay attention again, observing what kind of energy is being represented here and what, if anything, the figure may do or say in response to your scrutiny.

Repeat this exercise with the other two mirrors, one reflecting the connections you form with your friends and the other the connections you have with your work, your co-workers, your employees, your supervisors, and so forth, whatever is appropriate. Again, if a particular mirror does not really represent an important area of connection in your life, then feel free to rename it for another area of your choice.

When you have met the self reflected in each of the mirrors, turn back to the fifth, unlabeled mirror. As you do so, the reflections in each of the other mirrors step out and walk one by one into the fifth mirror. When they have done so, see who or what is reflected in that mirror. It will be an image that represents the co-incarnational you and the energy that this aspect of yourself holds for you.

As before, pay attention to this image. Most important, sense into the energy that it represents. Touch the mirror and draw this energy into yourself;

feel what it is like. Familiarize yourself with it so you may invoke it and draw its power into your life.

When you feel you are in touch with yourself and your energy as a being of pattern and not just of bodily form, then say thank you to the reflection and turn away. The mirrors will go blank, and the exercise is complete.

❧

As I said, the purpose of this exercise is not to identify all the connections that make up your pattern body or wide body. That would be nearly impossible, for it is fair to say that these connections can go on into infinity, though some are obviously stronger and more central than others. We each have connections to the land on which we live, the homes or buildings in which we live, and the things we own and use, as well as to people. If you want to expand this exercise to include these types of connections, feel free to do so. But remember that the objective is simply to have an experience of yourself as an embodied pattern and to feel what the energy of that is like.

❧

EXERCISE:
IMAGING THE PATTERN OF YOUR OBJECTIVE

A successful manifestation draws into your world not only the thing or person or condition itself but its co-incarnates as well. This is like marriage; you acquire not only a spouse but in-laws. If you are incompatible with your in-laws, this may not stop the marriage, but it is something that is good to know in advance so you are not shocked later.

In this exercise, you are going to draw a cluster diagram. Take a piece of blank paper. In the middle, write down the name of what it is you wish to manifest. Circle this name, and then draw another, larger circle around it. In this new circle, write down the qualities you would like associated with this manifestation. Then around these central circles, write down anything you can think of that is or might be connected to your objective, circling each item and connecting it by a line to the central circles. When you are finished, you will have a concrete image of the names of other things, places, conditions, feelings, symbols, images, persons, and so forth that you feel are connected to—co-incarnates of—your central desire.

Look this paper over, and without concentrating on any one element, get a feel for the whole perspective. What additional patterns or images emerge for you from contemplating the whole diagram?

Jot down on a separate sheet any impressions, images, or insights you have from doing this exercise. If what you experienced leads you to feel that there are implications or consequences to this manifestation that you are not comfortable with or do not wish, then this is valuable knowledge. You may then wish to end this manifestation project and go no further. Or you will proceed armed with the knowledge that you may encounter patterns that are not all you would choose.

For example, Julia would like to spend her summer vacation by the seashore. She thinks she would like to manifest a house to rent where she can do her own cooking, rather than eating in restaurants. To clarify the pattern of such a house, she creates the following cluster diagram.

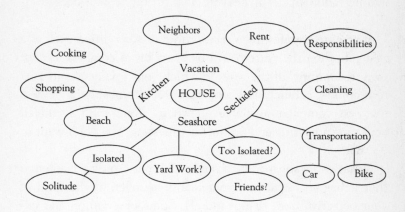

If you do decide to proceed, then the next step is to go further and explore how your pattern and that of your objective come together to create another link in the DNA of your new reality.

There are two ways to do this. One is to examine the implications of the consequences and new connections that your manifestation will bring into your life, as Julia did. How will these new connections match and blend with your own pattern life? Where might they be compatible and where incompatible?

Obviously, if you are manifesting a simple object, its pattern life is probably not going to be very complex. Consider the example of manifesting a car. If you are successful, you will draw into your life not only the automobile itself but its co-incarnates, which include driver's licenses, auto insurance, the petroleum industry in the form of gas and oil products, some degree of pollution, the need for a parking place or garage, the money for upkeep and repairs, registration fees, the scrutiny of police radars, and so forth. Owning a car is really taking on a particular lifestyle. If it is not a lifestyle you wish because it is in conflict with you and your pattern, then this may not be a manifestation made in heaven! It probably won't succeed either.

If you are manifesting a relationship or a condition such as a new job, then the pattern will be every bit as complex as your own. Examining all the ways in which your galaxy and its pattern collide, conflict, and cooperate would probably be beyond the best computer available anywhere. You would spend all your time analyzing and no time manifesting. You don't want to do that!

What you want is to be aware of this pattern dimension and that it has an impact on your reality as much as the form of your objective does (if not more!). Some observation and exploration can usually begin to show you where compatibilities and incompatibilities may lie, enough so that you can sense how this dimension will contribute to the kind of reality you will experience if your manifestation succeeds and whether that is a reality that you want.

However, what I am after here is something more than just analysis. I want you to tap into the spirit of this pattern dimension and use it as an ally to connect you with your manifestation. That is the thrust of this next exercise.

EXERCISE:
BLENDING THE PATTERNS

Imagine yourself floating in a featureless space that is warm, comforting, and safe. You can see clearly in all directions. There is no gravity; there are no currents to push or pull you one way or another. You might be in the sky, you might be underwater. It doesn't matter.

As you float, you become aware that you are not alone. In the distance something else is floating. It is the object of your manifestation.

You reach out to it, but it is just beyond your reach. Nor can you move over closer to it. All you can do is float where you are.

Now, visualize the energy or quality you felt when you attuned to the final figure in the five mirrors, the figure that represented your co-incarnational, pattern identity. Draw the reality of that part of you into yourself and around yourself.

Hold this image until you feel you have accomplished this.

When you feel attuned to the energy of your pattern self, you discover streams of light moving out from you toward that which you desire. These streams seem to arise from a company of beings around you, all those who share and are part of your pattern life. They arise from within you as well.

Like weaving strands of brilliant threads, these filaments reach for the object of your manifestation, but they are not quite able to reach it. Now call to your attention your awareness and insight into the pattern life of your manifestation. Feel into the reality and the energy of this pattern. When you feel you have a felt sense of this, call it to you.

As you do so, a similar cloud of threads reaches out from your objective toward you. These two clouds intertwine, pattern energy meeting pattern energy. As they do, you are pulled together.

What does this entwining and moving together feel like? Does it have a sensation, a color, a flavor, a sound? Does a symbol emerge, or any visual representation? How do you experience the quality of this contact and blending within yourself?

Take time to explore that feeling and commit it to your memory. If possible, feel it flooding into your body and moving through your cells, grounding itself into the memory and attunement of the physical.

When you feel you have a good sense of the energy of your patterns merging, imaginatively close your eyes, and you drop out of the space in which you were floating and land comfortably and easily into your body. The exercise ends.

The Seed Essence

I use the concept of essence as part of manifestation not for philosophical reasons. I use it because it is part of my experience. All the manifestations I have experienced have involved to a greater or lesser degree an element of spiritual energy. This energy seems to me to be part of all things, even artificial objects. For me, everything has interiority—an inner existence—and at its heart is a spiritual power. I call this power essence because it is as if all that something or someone has been, is, or can be is distilled into it. It individualizes the ground of all being and expresses a core identity that allows that something or someone to exist as a unique manifestation.

I invoke it in manifestation because I perceive it is there as a part of everything, and it seems rude to ask for the form of something to come into my life without inviting its essence or soul as well. That would be like asking someone to bring their body over for tea but to leave their mind at home (which is how many women feel men treat them anyway!).

Essence, soul, and *spirit* are all terms for a magical, miraculous, mysterious, and vital part of reality. If you are creating the seed of a new reality that you are going to manifest, this part needs to be included.

The question is how.

The fact is that the discernment and experience of essence is something that some people train for years to achieve (while other people seem to come by it naturally or have a knack for it). It is the product not of an exercise in a book but of an attunement practice, which may include meditation, prayer, ritual, and contemplation. It is an art in itself, a skill that is always maturing.

On the other hand, it does not take any training to be compassionate or loving, to open one's heart to another or to affirm each other as spiritual beings. By acting as if we were coming from our essence, which is loving and empowering, we build up our "essence-attunement muscles." We can play as if we were in touch with essence, and we will discover that we are. It is not all that mysterious, after all. The sacred breaks through to us in innumerable ways each day, I believe, and could do so even more if we paid more attention to the miraculousness and the wonderment of life.

One way of attuning to essence, which is very pertinent to manifestation, is to treat everyone and everything you encounter as if they and you were spiritual presences. By reaching out to their spiritual natures and by affirming your own, you establish a resonance that pulls that spirit into sharper focus. People begin to act to match your heightened perception of them. You begin to manifest a higher degree of spirit in your life.

You can have fun with this and treat it as a game. For one day, for example, pretend that you are an angel. If an angel is a radiant source of life-affirming, wisdom-nurturing, loving energy, how would you translate being that into actions and attitudes in your life? How would you seriously play at being a spiritual presence? (This is actually an exercise I give my students in classes on spirituality, but it can work just as well as part of the process of manifestation.)

In the case of your manifestation project, you give your objective a reality in your life by giving it respect, saluting the sacredness within it, and inviting its spiritual essence to be part of your life, which means you will treat it as something to be honored and not just as something to be acquired.

❧

Exercise:
Exploring Essence

In the myths and stories of many cultures, great heroes, wise men, and wise women often go through experiences of shape-shifting, during which they discover their true identity or their inner power. Like Merlin turning Arthur into a fish and a bird, these legendary figures experience what it would be like to be various kinds of creatures; yet throughout the course of their transmigration, something in them remains constant, the source of their true identity. In fact, some scholars suggest that these stories are illustrations of shamanic initiations, representing a training through which an individual discovers and attunes to his or her essence through discovering a consistency of inner identity in the midst of change.

In this simple exercise, which is as much of a conceptual adventure as a spiritual attunement, I want you to do something similar. You are going to attune to your essence by seeing what stays constant as you move imaginally through a series of forms.

Imagine yourself as an animal. What kind of animal would you be? What are the essential qualities of that animal, and how do they mirror your own qualities?

Now imagine yourself as a plant. What kind of plant would you be? What qualities would you embody? How does the essence of you as plant relate or compare to the essence of you as animal?

What if you were a song? What kind of a song would you be? What kind of dance? What essence of you is there, whether you are a song or a dance?

If you were a food, what would you be?

Give your self several different shapes and different identities, and ask who you would be in each instance. What is the essence of you that emerges from each of these identities? Or put another way, what is the common element that throws light on your essence?

When you are finished, repeat this exercise for the objective of your manifestation.

You can think of essence as a level of identity. It may also be seen as a condition of attunement. It is the part of you that can transcend the boundaries of self and attune to the communion of all being—the common spirit shared by all existence—and still retain a sense of individuality. It is the meeting place between the infinite unity on the one hand and the finite particularity of a specific identity on the other. It is the place where the wave and the particle meet and are one.

In this sense, using the image of boiling reality I offered in Chapter 4, essence is the transitional domain where a substance begins to precipitate out of a supersaturated solution. It is the first point of emergence. In thinking of the new reality you wish to precipitate in the form of your manifestation, essence is the condition or the point where that begins to happen. By attuning to the essence of your new reality, you call forth the point at which it truly begins to emerge within you and consequently within your world.

❧

EXERCISE:
THE BLENDING OF ESSENCE

Visualize the object of your manifestation. Imagine that it is slowly becoming transparent, and as it does so, you see a light glowing within it. As you watch, this light grows brighter while the actual form grows dimmer, until all you can see is the light itself.

Walk into this light. Stand in it for a while, and let its nature wash over and through you. What does it feel like? What qualities does it evoke in you? What is its energy like? What is its presence like?

You then step out of this light and turn around. You are now looking at yourself. Like the object of your manifestation, you, too, are becoming transparent and glowing with an inner light. Step into this light and feel its qualities, its energy, its presence.

When you are satisfied that you have attuned to this essence and have a sense of its nature, turn back to the light glowing from within the objective of your manifestation. Remaining in your own essence, walk over to it and into it, blending the two essences together. Feel their light interpenetrating each other. What is that like? Does it spark any images, thoughts, or feelings?

Spend some time in the midst of this combined essence. Become familiar with what it feels like. When you feel you are finished, close your inner eyes and open your outer ones. The exercise is ended.

The Seed and Unity

No connections need be formed at the level of unity because by definition at that level you and your objective are already one. This is easy to experience when you are at the wavelike level of unity within yourself but harder when you are in your particular, personal, everyday identity, wishing you had something that you don't. Oneness may then seem too abstract to be useful. After all, being one with a toaster I don't yet possess is not going to give me hot toast in the morning!

On the other hand, manifestation is about unfolding something from within rather than trying to attract something from the outside. In the previous chapter, I used the image of gardening to convey this idea. I may not have my carrots yet, but I can grow them in my soil. However, if I don't have the soil, I won't have the carrots either.

Unity is the soil from which we all spring. Experiencing that unity in yourself gives you a place to plant the seed of your desired reality. Put another way, holding the image of the oneness you have with that which you seek to manifest is a far richer and more potent source of energy with which to begin your manifestation project than holding an image of lack and separation.

Exploring the condition of unity is a lifetime spiritual practice all on its own. The value of experiencing unity extends far beyond its role in the art of manifestation, for it is the place from which unconditional compassion and love—a sense of oneness with and caring for our fellow creatures and for all the world—may emerge. It is the sacred center toward which all spiritual and religious paths converge. Having a spiritual practice that allows you to explore unity in a disciplined way is an inestimable aid and resource in pursuing this inner art.

In the meditative, contemplative, mystical, and spiritual traditions of humanity, there are many techniques and practices for experiencing the unitive state. Here are two simple exercises to get you started and give you a flavor of this goal. Beyond this, I suggest further exploration in one or more of those traditions according to your preferences.

Exercise:
Exploring Unity

Begin by imagining yourself a spring of pure water bubbling out between rocks high on a mountainside. You emerge as a very thin stream of water running down the slope. Picture yourself as this stream, not very wide, bounded by rocks and grass and soil.

As you move down the mountain, however, you begin to get larger. Your boundaries begin to widen. Your speed begins to increase. You connect and merge with other small streams and rivulets, becoming still wider. Now, where a rock might have blocked your passage before, you flow over it.

Cascading down the mountain, you pick up speed

and volume. At one point you leap over a cliff, your water sparkling in the sunlight, rainbows dancing in your spray. You surge down gorges, your water foaming and dancing, feeling your power and the delight in your journey. Sometimes rocky walls hem you in, and you travel faster; other times you spread out, carving your way through the countryside.

Eventually you reach the valley. You spread out even more. You pass through meadows and pastures, past farms and villages. In the distance, you can see a city. Mighty bridges strain to span your width as you approach the sea. Feel the kind of river you are. Feel your boundaries, your banks, the current of your flow.

Then you come to the end of the land. You enter the ocean. Feel yourself being swept into the sea. Your boundaries drop away. You are no longer a river, separate from all other rivers. You and all the other rivers merge, become one in the sea. Feel the boundlessness of this new condition. Feel its depth. No longer a river, you are the ocean. Many currents move through you in many directions. You are everywhere. What does this feel like? What is its felt sense in your body?

Enjoy being the ocean for a while; then when you complete this imaginative exercise, record any particular thoughts, sensations, feelings, or images that may have come to you.

SECOND EXERCISE

Here is a variation on the preceding exercise. Imagine yourself a beach. (If you have ever visited a beach, try to remember it in its particulars to help you in this exercise.) How long are you? How wide are you? Does the sea roll smoothly and sedately over your sand, or does the surf crash down upon you? Do you have tidal pools? If so, what kind of life lives in them? In short, imagine yourself as a very specific beach with specific characteristics.

Now let your imagination flow into the ocean, whose waves caress you. As you become the ocean, you look back at the specific beach that you were, but now you become aware of many other beaches. All around you, you touch uncounted beaches, all of them different, each unique, but each a beach because it is connected to you. Some are thin, some are fat, some are rocky, some are sandy, some are rough, some are smooth, but all of the beaches are connected to you. And in you, each beach connects with every other beach. Feel yourself as the ocean that touches and connects all the beaches of the world.

What does it feel like to be a particular beach? What does it feel like to be the ocean that connects all beaches? Write down any images, sensations, ideas, and so forth that this exercise brings up for you, but most important, seek to gain a felt sense of what the state of being an ocean—of being unity— is like with respect to the beaches.

The Heart of the Matter: Reality and the New You

I want to be clear about what you are doing next, for this is the heart of your project. Forgive me if I repeat here some of what I have said earlier in the book.

For something to manifest, there must be a felt sense of its reality, a seed around which it can coalesce.

If this seed is not there, your manifestation will remain ungrounded and abstract, its energy unable to fully connect with you or your current reality. Then you may end up dealing with fantasy and wishful thinking.

The more the nature of the seed corresponds to the holistic nature of reality, the more potent it is. Reality is a spectrum of being ranging from the most dense, particularized, material form to the most rarefied, wavelike, cosmic spirit and on into the mystery of the sacred. Therefore, the wider the range the seed can contain, the more vitality and substance it will have and the more it can embody that felt sense of reality.

This is why I have you practice deep and holistic visualization rather than just surface visualization. You want to gather into your vision more of the ranges of existence than just the level of form.

Form, pattern, essence, and unity are simply four markers upon the spectrum, representing major transition points from one phase of the whole to another. What is important, though, is not specific information about each of these states but an experience of the reality of the spectrum itself in its wholeness. In particular, you want to experience and internalize a felt sense of the reality of that spectrum as it will exist within your particular manifestation.

I have been calling this felt sense various things: the new reality, the seed image, and even the "new you." Clarifying this felt sense is the final stage of this part of your manifestation project. It is what we are going to next. This felt sense *is* the seed of reality around which your manifestation will occur.

There must be a point of emergence where this seed first appears and becomes a field of living, unfolding energy.

You are that point of emergence. Specifically, it begins in your imagination. For human beings, imagination is the womb of reality. All that exists for us in our human world began in someone's imagination.

However, this seed in you is more than just an imaginative image to hold before your mind's eye. It is a presence that you inhabit, like a new house that you are going to fill with your belongings and turn into a home. You do not just visualize. You embody. The seed becomes more than a seed. It is a field of energy through which you express. It is a body for the fulfillment of your manifestation. It is the body of what you will become as a result of your manifestation.

When you manifest, you are manifesting a new identity, a new you.

When you apply this inner art, you are manifesting two things. You are manifesting the specific objective you have in mind, which, unless it is an inner state such as greater peace or a personal condition such as greater health, is something separate from you. You are also manifesting a new condition in which the object of your manifestation has become part of your life along with whatever changes it may bring. You are manifesting a new condition of self, a new you.

The importance of this distinction is that it is easier to achieve a felt sense of reality about a new condition within yourself than about a car that doesn't exist in your driveway, a job that you don't go to yet, or a relationship you don't have. This distinction—the whole idea of the "new you"—is simply a tool. Which seems to you to be easier to manifest: a new job or a new you? A new car or a new you? A new relationship or a new you? Both may seem equally challenging, but an interior state is easier to imagine and induce and can carry a deeper sense of reality than the image of an outer form that doesn't exist yet.

Furthermore, and this is very important, an inner state is more than an image; it is an experience. You can experience yourself; you cannot experience something that you don't have. An inner experience is already a reality, not an abstraction, a wish, or a dream. It is not just something in your mind. It exists now in your feelings and in your body as well. It is already a part of your current reality. Because this is so, it can be the fulcrum around which your current reality shifts and transforms.

With proper nourishment and connections, this inner experience can be the seed from which the reality of your manifestation grows.

The new you may be significantly different from the old you or pretty much the same. Manifesting a new pair of shoes is not going to change you as much as manifesting a house (unless, of course, they are a fabulously comfortable pair of shoes!). But the degree of difference is not the issue. It is the quality of being different that counts. It is the way in which the old you and the new you are different that you are manifesting. It is this difference that you wish to bring about.

The Seed Image

You have traced the strands of identity that make up the double helix—the DNA—of your manifestation. You have a sense of how you and your objective entwine and interact to create a field of energy and potential between you. Now you must take one more step and use this metaphysical DNA to create a seed image of the new you that you can take into yourself and embody. You have the genetic material, so to speak. It is time to create the offspring.

⋙⋘

Exercise:
Creating the Seed Image

Imagine yourself outdoors in a peaceful natural setting, standing before a table. On it are four boxes and a large empty cauldron or pot. Next to the cauldron is a large, ornate golden stirring spoon.

The four boxes are labeled. One box is labeled "Form," one is labeled "Pattern," the third is labeled "Essence," and the last is labeled "Unity."

Open the box labeled "Form." In it is the quality of reality you experienced when you did the exercise on blending your form with that of your objective. Take time to remember what it felt like.

Reach your hand in and grasp this reality, observing what it may feel like or any form that it takes in your hands. Take it out of the box and put it into the cauldron.

Now open the box labeled "Pattern." In it is the quality of reality you experienced when you did the exercise on blending your pattern identity with that of your objective. Take time to remember what it felt like.

Reach your hand in and grasp this reality, observing what it may feel like or any form that it takes. Take it out of the box and put it into the cauldron.

Next open the box labeled "Essence." As in the

boxes you have opened, it contains the felt sense of a particular reality, in this case that which you experienced when you did the exercise on blending your essences together. Take time to remember what this reality felt like.

Now reach your hand in and grasp this reality, observing what it may feel like or any form that it takes. Take it out of the box and put it into the cauldron.

Finally, open the last box, which is labeled "Unity." In it is the quality of reality you experienced when you attuned to the unitive state within you. Take time to remember what it felt like.

Reach your hand in and grasp this reality, observing what it may feel like or any form that it takes. Take it out of the box and put it into the cauldron.

You now have all the genetic components in the cauldron. Take the golden stirring spoon and stir it all up. As you do so, the mixture begins to glow and give off light, which begins to expand within the cauldron.

When the light fills the cauldron, stop stirring. Lift the cauldron and place it on the ground, then step back from it.

As you watch, the light becomes a sphere enveloping the cauldron, which disappears. This sphere then explodes upward in a great column of brilliance, with even brighter strands of light within it swirling about each other like a double helix, reaching from the earth and vanishing into the heavens. You can sense and feel forces moving up and down along this column of light.

Abruptly, the light disappears. In its place stands a glowing figure. This is, you recognize, the new you.

It is you as you will be when your manifestation succeeds.

The two of you move toward each other, first embracing, then merging. Feel this glowing being entering into you. What does it feel like? How is it different from you? What is the nature of that difference?

At this point, visualize this figure as yourself, or you as this figure. Affirm its reality within you. Pay attention to what that reality feels like in your body, in your thoughts, in your feelings, in your subtle or spiritual nature. How does its energy sit within you? Note any sensations that arise. How do you feel different from before?

Remember, it is this sense of difference, this sense of the reality of this new you within you that you will be using as the focal point for your manifestation. It is what you are manifesting. Be as clear as you can about how you experience it, and make it as real as you can to every level of your being.

When you have done this, look down at the ground. There you may see an object or a symbol that has been left there by your new you as it merged with you. This object or symbol represents this new you and its reality within you. If there is no object or symbol, then you can ask that one appear, but if nothing does, then you do not need it, and it is not important.

At this point, close your inner eyes and open your outer eyes. Move about your room and try to maintain the sense of the energy of the new you within yourself. The exercise is over.

You have finished with the genetics of your manifestation. You have created a seed state within you. Remember that at any time you wish, you can go back and do any of these exercises again to reinforce the experience for yourself and to make it more clear and present for you.

Now you are ready for the last two steps in the process, which are the inner and outer nourishing, energizing, and unfolding of the new you.

Chapter Eight

Boiling Reality

In Chapter 4, "The Energy of Miracles," I talked about investigating my experiences with manifestation to see what happens at that moment when reality seems to shift. I spoke about perceiving a heightening of energy within my reality and the appearance of a holistic aspect of myself that I called presence. When this happens, my attachment to things as they are is loosened, reality becomes more wavelike and expanded, and an opening is created for new connections to form and a new reality to appear. To sum up this experience, I used the image of "boiling" reality.

I have used that experience to develop a manifestation ritual as the next step in your project.

At this point, you have a seed image of the reality you wish to manifest in the form of an experience of a new you. Now you want to invoke energy and life from your holistic presence to flow into and inhabit that image, expanding it, vitalizing it, and giving it the power to act as an organizing force within your life, attracting coincidences, synchronicities, connections, insights, and whatever else may be needed to bring your manifestation into being.

This invocation and energizing of the new you is the function of the manifestation ritual. I call it a ritual because it is something you do periodically on a regular basis, and it has some elements that you repeat each time you do it.

For the first three or four times you do this, I suggest you follow this ritual closely, paying attention to its flow and to the quality of spirit and energy you are feeling at each stage. This is to enable you to gain familiarity with what you are doing and why. After that, as with other elements of your manifestation project, feel free to adapt this ritual to meet your particular needs. What I am offering is more in the way of suggestions than techniques you must use. If you understand the process and its intent, then you can create your own ritual or even, in time, dispense with this ritual altogether as you discover that you can move in and out of your presence at will and focus the energy of that presence when it is needed. (Since it is a source of love and blessing, you can invoke your presence at other times and for other needs than simply as part of a manifestation project. Making a habit of bringing its energy and quality into your everyday life can have a powerful effect of enriching and deepening your personal reality.)

To perform this ritual, you should set aside about an hour when you can be undisturbed. Ideally, you should do this in the same place each time so that you establish a rhythm of familiarity. You do not want to become obsessive about your manifestation, always wondering when it is going to come about and thinking about it too much; however, I recommend doing this ritual three times a week the first week of your project and at least once a week thereafter.

You will want to have a candle. You may also wish to have a

writing pad, pen or pencil, a drawing pad, and some colored pens, paints, or crayons, and some small stones or crystals, should you wish to write, draw, color, or create talismanic objects as part of the ritual.

You may find it helpful to read completely through the ritual process before actually doing it. It includes my own example of going through a sample ritual as well as instructions, descriptions, and commentary on the process.

Sacred Space

All rituals take place in sacred space. Such a space may be dedicated to being a place of attunement, like a chapel or synagogue, or even the prayer rug of a Moslem. It can also be created in the moment through setting up boundaries of time and space and performing an appropriate invocation. That is what you will now do.

Set aside a space for your working. It does not have to be a large space, but it should have room for you to move about should you need to, as well as to sit quietly on the floor or in a chair. There should be room for five candles and for any writing and drawing tools you have brought with you.

To do this ritual, you are going to be sitting or standing in a circle. The circle is an ancient symbol of wholeness and connectedness, and it is often used to delineate a sacred space. You do not actually have to draw a circle on the floor; it is sufficient for you to visualize it in your mind's eye. However, to help you, put a candle at each of the four directions: east, south, west, and north. Then you can imagine the circumference of the circle joining these four candles.

There is another reason for marking the four directions. A compass is a tool for locating yourself (or anything) in space. For something to exist upon the earth, it does so in a specific place which can be defined in terms of directional coordinates. You are seeking to manifest something physically upon the earth. (Even if your objective is an inner state within you, your body still inhabits a specific place upon the earth.) So a circle defined by the four directions of the compass is like a portal into the material dimension; it is a symbol of being located in space. By its very nature, it symbolizes forces of physical incarnation and attunes your manifestation project to their gifts of physical dimension. It also strengthens your inner sense that you are giving physical existence to your manifestation.

Visualizing the circle and marking it with four candles constitutes establishing the physical boundaries of your sacred space.

The fifth candle you will place in the center of the circle. It will mark the temporal boundaries of your sacred space. When you light this candle, the ritual begins; you have entered into a special creative time set apart from the ordinary activities of your day. When you blow it out, the ritual is over. You lower the boundaries and let the special time flow out, to be reunited with ordinary time. You are ready to return to your daily activities.

Invocation

Having defined your sacred space, you now activate it through invocation.

> To begin any ritual, I light a candle. As well as being a way of signaling that the ritual has begun, a candle also has a spiritual meaning for me, representing the invocation of light, the guidance of spirit, and the creative power within all things.
> As I light my candle, I say words of invocation: "With this flame I invoke into this time and place the creative spirit of

God, the Beloved, the fire that empowers all manifestations, the light that can guide my spirit into deeper wisdom and attunement. I invoke the blessing of this spirit and its light upon myself, my manifestation, and upon my world at large.''

You should feel free, of course, to find your own words and thoughts of invocation or not to use any at all if doing so would seem strange and unnatural to you. However, since you are attuning to one of the formative powers in the universe and to its deep creative and organizing spirit, some acknowledgment seems appropriate and can put you into an enlarged frame of mind.

I then activate the sacred space by lighting the four candles around the edge of my imaginary circle. Though these mark only four directions, all ritual work and sacred space is actually defined by seven directions: the four compass directions symbolizing physical existence; above representing spiritual forces and dimensions; below representing the vital forces of the earth on which we live; and within representing our own inner spirit and presence. So after acknowledging the four directions, I then inwardly acknowledge and attune to these other three directions that define me and that will also define the new me that will emerge from the manifestation.

Silence

Now I take time simply to sit in silence and quiet myself. All things emerge from creative silence. Think of a seed deep within the soil in the warm, nourishing, quiet darkness. I am the soil for my manifestation.

Silence in this sense is not necessarily an absence of noise or sound. It is really an absence of distraction or confusion. It is the transformation of scattered, jagged energy into a calm, smooth, rhythmic flow within yourself.

There are many meditative and contemplative techniques for practicing silence, and you should seek out the method that works for you. I find simply monitoring my breath—witnessing the rhythm of my breathing in and breathing out—and making my breath rhythmic through an act of gentle will, helps in taking me into that silence.

> *Within silence, I begin to withdraw my attention from the energies of time and space. I detach myself by entering into no-thing-ness. I call back into myself all the parts of my psyche that I have scattered out into the world through my thoughts and feelings, my plans, my desires, my worries, my fears, and so forth. I recollect myself and center myself so I can be wholly present to the spirit in this moment.*

Embrace Current Reality

Current reality has its own integrity, its own momentum, its own incarnation, which you must honor.

In your manifestation project, you seek to change your current reality in some manner. Paradoxically, you do this by embracing it and attuning to it more deeply, not by denying it. This is because whatever the content of your reality, it is also a source of energy. It embodies the same forces of incarnation and existence that you want to use for your manifestation.

You may not like your current reality, but it has an integrity that you must respect and honor. If you attune to it properly by accepting and acknowledging your responsibility in creating it and how it reflects your choices in life, then it lends you its energy. It becomes an ally. If you simply reject it or deny any personal responsibility for the shape it is in, it can be an obstacle. You wish your manifestation to become real, but you cannot help that happen if you are rejecting reality.

Furthermore, in this ritual you are seeking to energize your current reality to make it more fluid and open to change; you are going to lift it up like a chalice to be filled with the spirit and blessing of the sacred and of your own inner presence. You can hardly do that if you are also rejecting and denying that reality and refusing to see it as it is. You must embrace your reality in order to transform it. If it is a painful reality, just remember that Jesus healed the lepers not by turning away from them but by embracing them and cleaning their wounds. Engagement, not denial, is the key to transformation.

Peter Caddy used to teach at Findhorn that one of the most transforming things you could do within your present reality was to love whom you are with, what you are doing, and where you are. I have always found this to be true. Again, aside from the healing and transforming power of love itself, there is nothing I can do to change my reality if I am emotionally or mentally running away from it or in conflict with it.

I am still in silence, cultivating detachment, pulling my energy into my center. Once I feel centered, though, I turn my attention to my current reality. I do not attempt to analyze it or list all the things that are right or wrong. I simply look upon my life and the state of my affairs, and let any images that will arise before my inner vision. Whatever comes forth, though, I embrace in love and the spirit of peacefulness and let it go.

After a few moments of just letting these images rise up spontaneously, I now call to my attention any particular elements or conditions in my life that trouble me and keep me from fully embracing the reality of my life, especially if they relate to my manifestation. From my detached and peaceful place, I project love to these troubling elements. I do not try to change them, understand them, or fix them. I am simply observing them and not allowing them to fill me with denial or to lessen my attunement to my current reality. I embrace them so that I can then freely embrace the whole of my reality with all its pattern and contents.

Through this loving embrace I draw the wholeness and energy of this reality into my sacred space, leaving no part, no matter how troubling, fearsome, or shameful, outside the circle. In this way, I bring all of myself together within the circle in preparation for invoking presence and for expanding my current reality with the energy of my seed image, which is a reality-in-waiting.

Attune to Coincidence and Miracle

After drawing your awareness of your current reality into the circle of the ritual, it is time to get your reality dancing by sprinkling it with a pinch of magic and a dash of miracles.

You do this by attuning to coincidences. Remember that I called coincidences "little miracles." You can attune to miracles, too, but coincidences seem more homey and accessible. Big miracles seem to happen only now and again, perhaps only once in a person's lifetime, but little miracles happen almost every day. Appreciating this heightens your sense of the active presence of a "miracle-making" activity at work in the world. It can strengthen your awareness that this activity is accessible and available.

The objective is to heighten your mood by contemplating the wonderment and power contained within miracles and coincidences, which leads naturally to considering the wonder and power embodied in creation and in the sacred. This in turn attunes you to the sacred, which is where you want to be.

So think of any coincidences that have occurred in your life or in the lives of people you know. Or you may wish to think about miracles and coincidences you have read about, such as in the Bible or in modern books such as Don Wakefield's *Expect a Miracle*. The ideal, though, is to think of miracles and coincidences in your own life, for these will have a reality for you. As much as you can throughout your manifestation project, you want to align what you are doing with your personal sense of reality. So consider what you are doing here as invoking an awareness of the miraculous side of your reality, for it is that side you are expecting to give flesh to the new you.

Sitting in silence after embracing my sense of my current reality into my sacred circle, I begin to think about the energy of miracles at work in the world. It is that energy I wish to invoke. One way is to think of coincidences and miracles I have experienced or that I know about.

In this instance, I recall a recent phone conversation with my mother. She called to tell me a manifestation story. The church she attends had purchased new hymnals. The old ones had been stacked by the exit, and the minister announced that any member of the congregation who wished to have one could just pick one up on the way out.

As she left the church, my mother stopped to pick up a hymnal for her older sister who because of illness was no longer able to attend services. The first one that she picked up had been damaged, so she put it back, rummaged around quickly in the pile of books, then drew one out whose cover looked fairly decent. "I wasn't paying much attention to what I was do-ing," she told me. "I was just letting my fingers find the book they wanted."

Later on the way home, my mother took time to examine more closely the book she had picked up for her older sister. To her astonishment and delight, when she opened it she saw on the title page an official statement saying that this hymnal had been purchased for the church by her older sister as a memorial to her husband. Out of the hundreds of old hymnals that her church was giving away, my mother had randomly chosen the one book that would mean the most to her sister—the very one my aunt had donated to the church many years previously!

Thinking about this story fills me with delight. It fills me with a sense of possibility and of the magic of life. It is exactly this same possibility and magic I am depending on to enable my manifestation to happen.

This story reminds me that we all live in a sea of miracles, most of which we never notice. I draw energy from this image, an energy of excitement, wonder, and possibility. I can feel this energy as a stirring in my body, a lightening of my mind and heart, a joy within my spirit. This growing energy of delight and creativity is exactly what I wish to invoke as part of this ritual.

Attune to Spirit and the Sacred

One day when I was a child living in Morocco, my father gave me a magnifying glass and took me outside onto the driveway. It was a hot clear day with no clouds in the sky. The sun was bright and fierce overhead. My father took some grass from the lawn and laid it in a small pile on the concrete. "Now, son," he said, "use your magnifying glass to focus the light of the sun onto that grass." To my delight, I discovered that when I angled the lens just right, I could see a bright spot on the grass where a beam of sunlight was being concentrated. Then, as I watched, the grass began to smoke, then burst into flame. In hardly any time, the small pile was on fire.

When you undertake a manifestation project, you are heightening and focusing a creative process, like using a magnifying glass to focus sunlight to produce a concentrated beam. But before you can use a lens, before there can be a beam, there must first be sunlight, and you must be in it.

In this case, the sunlight is the light of the higher spiritual worlds of essence and unity whose continual radiance brings energy and blessing. It is also the presence of the sacred. You now need to open yourself to that mystery and to your own transpersonal levels. It is these levels that have the power to boil your reality.

Because attunement to the spiritual dimensions is such a personal area, you must determine for yourself just how you will do this. Every religious or spiritual tradition has its own way of calling upon the sacred, and you may find one or another more powerful and meaningful for you.

In my own case, I use a variation on the Christian mystical tradition of Centering Prayer. This consists of thinking of the Beloved (my term for God) as It manifests in my life and in creation as a whole. My response to this thought is always one of joy and love. I let that response build within me while keeping my thoughts centered on my image of the Beloved until I feel my being filled with the love and presence of the sacred.

Once I feel attuned to the sacred, I often reach out in my heart to connect with a spiritual "ally." An ally represents either an inner personal image or a nonphysical spiritual friend or contact whose energy can assist you both in attuning to higher spiritual realms and in fulfilling your manifestation project. The use of spiritual allies is a major technique in shamanic and magical practices. In the form of praying to angels, saints, and other god-infused or spiritual beings, it is also consistent with traditional religious practices. The key point to remember is that the ally is not a being who will get what you want for you or do the manifestation for you. The function of the ally is to empower you with information, insight, and energy to accomplish your objective yourself. The ally is a friendly supporter, not a parent upon whom you can be dependent.

Allies can take many forms. They can be historical figures, angelic beings, even animals. Keep in mind that the ally makes contact with you and empowers you through your imagination. Thus the energy of the ally can be clothed in whatever form most resonates with your imagination. Part of the discipline and training in working with such allies is learning to see past the form in which they appear to your mind's eye (since you may be creating that form, drawing on religious, literary, or historical imagery to do so) and attuning to the essential quality of their spirit. Also, the function of the ally is not to make you attached in any way to itself but to infuse your creative presence with energy, integrity, and wholeness.

There are many ways of contacting an ally. Prayer is a traditional and simple way. Ritual can also be used. I use the technique of storytelling to help in this area. This would be a story about connecting with a source of inner wisdom and insight. Here is an example, but you should feel free to develop stories that are unique and meaningful to you.

EXERCISE:
CONTACTING A SPIRITUAL ALLY

Visualize the following: You are sitting in your room when you hear a knock on the door. You get up and open the door. To your surprise, instead of the familiar setting on the other side, you find yourself looking out on a beautiful woodland scene. Sunlight is shining through a grove of ancient trees, and you hear the sound of bird song in the leaves. Beside the grove is a stone well, partly in shade, partly in sunshine.

Standing by the door is a hooded figure, fully robed in a loose green garment. You cannot tell whether it is a man or a woman, but there emanates from this person such a gentle and loving feeling that you are immediately at ease. The figure turns toward the well and beckons you to follow. If you choose to do so, you step through the door. If you decide not to do so, the door closes and you return to your chair and the story ends.

If you follow the figure, you approach the well. The hooded figure indicates you should look into it. When you do, you see that the water is as clear as a mirror. As you look, an image appears that gives you information about yourself and your manifestation. Take note of what this image is, and remember what it has to tell you.

When the image clears, you look up. Now the figure has removed its hood, and you can see whether it is a man or a woman. You may then ask this figure a question about your manifestation, and he or she will answer. The answer may come in the form of words or symbols or ideas in your mind. Take note of what it is.

Now the figure reaches into a pocket in his or her robe and draws something out. This is a gift to empower you and your manifestation. The figure hands this gift to you, and you take it. Take note of what it is and what it does, if anything.

The figure now beckons you back toward the door into your room. You walk past the grove of trees and

pass through the door. As you do so, you feel a blessing from the trees, the well, and the figure and an
invitation to return should you need to. Then the
door closes. You return to your chair and sit down
and your story ends.

Now take some paper and write down or, if necessary, draw anything that you saw or heard on this
journey. Take note of any images, feelings, or
thoughts that arise in you as a result of participating
in this story.

Stories like this provide an opening for images and thoughts
to arise from deeper levels of consciousness. They can be very
helpful and informative. On the other hand, you must still use
your discernment and good judgment in evaluating the material
you receive. As with a dream, valuable insights can emerge, but
you can't always take everything literally or at face value, and
some form of interpretation may be necessary.

Though you have created this manifestation project and are
doing this ritual because of a desire, when you attune to the
transpersonal realms, desire falls away. It is part of your personal
life but not necessarily part of your transpersonal being. This in
no way means the desire was wrong, only that its energy has no
meaning on transpersonal levels. When you touch the realms
where oneness and unity are fundamental characteristics of experience, there is nothing to desire, at least not in a manner
understandable to the personality's perspective. How can the
particle understand the wave? The particle seeks out other particles, for that is its nature, but the wave is the other particles
already.

Entering into the domain of the higher spirit, you come into a place of unconditionality. Here the response is not to say, "This is what I want!" The response is to move unconditionally to be in the presence of the sacred, which is the source of all things. It is to allow that source to act within and upon you unconditionally, trusting that it knows what you need more precisely and lovingly than you do yourself.

I center myself in my love for the Beloved and in the joy that fills my life because of the blessings of the sacred. Contemplating the Beloved, I feel myself moving beyond my personality and into the essence of my spirit. In this place, I have no desire. I am nourished simply by being there, and that is sufficient. I take some time just to sit with this feeling of unity. With every breath, I breathe in the spirit of the Beloved. I fill my cells with light and unconditional love. I attune myself to source. Manifestation can wait!

Engage in Blessing: Being an Angel

For a time, you may simply wish to be in the presence of your transpersonal self and the presence of the sacred, breathing in a spirit of blessing and peace, love and grace.

The next step is to be a source yourself—to be an angel, so to speak. The best way to engage with the vibrant radiant energies of the transpersonal realms is to do what those energies do: radiate vibrantly!

This means that you turn your attention outward to the world (not just your personal world but all the world) and begin to bless it. In your heart's eye, see love and blessing radiate from you as streamers of light. Think of yourself as turning yourself inside out, for inside you is light and love and joy, so let it spill out of you, overflow from you, and rush into the world.

If you wish, you can direct this light to particular conditions or areas of the world where you feel it is needed. You may direct it to people.

However, your primary task in this context and within this ritual is to give your light and energy to the overall evolution and creative unfoldment of the world and of all life upon it. Like the Bodhisattva in Buddhist philosophy, you are giving from yourself to increase the level of enlightenment in the world as a whole. This is a fundamental task as a human being: to increase the presence of light and love in the world and to enhance attunement to the loving, creative, transforming spirit of the sacred. This is the planetary manifestation project, to give birth to a new heaven and a new earth, to manifest a world of wholeness and delight.

> *I open to receive the presence of the Beloved into my being. As it flows into my heart, I gather this light, this love, this joy, and direct it back into my world. Where there is suffering, I visualize comfort and healing; where there is hatred, I visualize love; where there is shatteredness, I visualize wholeness and regeneration. Where there is foolishness, I visualize wisdom. I see in my heart the places where the world groans and people cry out, and into those places I focus my spirit to be a channel for the grace and compassion of the Beloved.*
>
> *I see all the world as a great being unfolding in its consciousness and spirit. I see a vision of a sacred world, one in which humanity, nature, and spirit are united and work co-creatively, cooperatively, and with mutual benefit. I offer my life and my energy toward the manifestation of this world.*
>
> *I make myself an instrument through which the Beloved may give blessings to the world.*

Invoke Presence and Boil Reality

Out of this state of blessing and participation in the enlightenment of the world, I turn again in my mind's eye toward my own being. I align with my body, with my psyche, with my pattern of relationships, with my essence, as well as with unity. I hold all these parts of me in my heart and feel their oneness. I appreciate the whole range of my being, from personality to oneness—from particle to wave—and in that appreciation, I invoke my presence. I invoke the power, the playfulness, the humor of my creative self in all its wholeness.

I feel it within me. More important, I feel it as me. I am my presence. How could it be otherwise? It is not something separate from me. It is me when I expand to express through as much of the human spectrum of being as I can imagine or understand.

As presence, I turn my attention on my current reality and I bless it, I enter into it, I inhabit it. As if it were water in a pot, I see it begin to boil. I see it begin to dance, to shimmer, to vibrate. I look to see where the stuck places, the shadowed places, the weary places may be and direct extra energy in their direction. I see my body, my house, the things I own, and the land where I live all filling with this dancing light, beginning to vibrate faster and faster, like water molecules in a pot on a hot stove. I visualize my personal world raising its energy, beginning to boil.

This is the stage where you invoke and inhabit your presence, filling your life and world with its dynamic, playful, creative energy. Think back to the exercises you did in the last chapter on attuning to the reality of your form, pattern, essence, and unity. The blending of these is your presence; it is your wholeness in action. What does that feel like? Make it as real for yourself as you can.

Energize the Seed of the New You

Now that you are in a heightened state, in touch with your presence and the higher spiritual energies of life, it is time to bring forward your seed image. Recall all the work you did to create that image. Remember the felt sense of its reality within you. You are going to energize and expand that felt sense. You are going to bless that image. You are going to give it substance.

There are several ways of doing this. The object is to fill this seed image with spiritual energy and to align it with the flow of spirit into matter, as well as to continue to enhance your sense of its reality.

You can align it with your own transpersonal love and will and with service.

USING TRANSPERSONAL LOVE. Loving that which you wish to manifest and, by extension, the new self that will result as a consequence of that manifestation, is not the same as desiring it. Chances are you already desire the objective of your manifestation. Loving it, though, in a transpersonal sense, means infusing it with energies of empowerment, goodwill, and love whether you get it or not; it means loving it for itself in order to acknowledge and affirm its higher potentials.

One challenge of desire is that once fulfilled, the energy or passion that connected us to that which we desired goes away. We are left with something we possess, but we may not be in creative partnership with it. That is, it is no longer a conduit for our creative energy. It can in fact, as many possessions and outworn conditions do, become a block for that energy.

The metaphor I think of is courtship and marriage. A romantic passion infuses courtship. But often that energy fades away once a couple is married, its passion leached out of the relationship by increasing familiarity. Of course, successful marriages may keep that romantic fire alive, but what really supports a creative relationship is a love that goes deeper than surface excitement and the fulfillment of desire. This is the love that sustains a couple "for better for worse," through exciting times and dry times. It is a love that is in it for the long haul and is willing to go deeply into those realms of mutual learning and transformation that are so much a part of any successful long-term marriage or friendship.

Now, many things that you may wish to manifest are not intended for the long haul. Manifesting a new sofa or the month's rent or even a new job is not the same as making a lifelong commitment in a marriage. However, once the blaze of desire is fulfilled, will you lose interest and, in doing so, become neglectful of those acts of caring and attentiveness that honor and maintain that which you have manifested? Love is an antidote to the kind of familiarity that breeds forgetfulness, neglect, and the hunger for new sensation, new passions, and new conquests. This is as true in a relationship with a toaster as with a spouse.

More to the point, what you are manifesting is a new aspect or expression of yourself. How mindful, powerful, energetic, and whole do you wish this new aspect to be? Simply acquiring things or conditions does not increase your power or your mindfulness; it does not enable you to inhabit yourself or your life well. What does do so is the degree to which you can love the new you that you are manifesting and through that love be alert and true to your higher nature "for better for worse." So while you may not be marrying the house you manifested, you are marrying the you that will live in it—or more precisely, the deeper you or soul that all the conditions of your life ultimately serve either to reveal or to obscure, depending on the mindfulness and love with which you relate to them.

EXERCISE:
WELCOMING THE NEW YOU WITH LOVE

Sitting in silence and with a clear sense of the new you that you wish to manifest, embrace that image with love. Imagine some person or condition that truly inspires you with a selfless love. What does that love feel like? Embrace the new you with this feeling of love. Draw it into your being, into your heart, and welcome it into your life with this lovingness. As you do so, imagine this love expanding and connecting you and that which you wish to manifest with the unconditional love of the sacred, the love at the heart of all creation. Hold this feeling as long as it feels comfortable, and then relax, breathing this energy of love out to all the world, into your manifestation, and into your life as it is in the moment. When you have done this, you have completed this exercise.

Love is the most attractive and magnetic power in creation, especially when it is selfless and empowering, acting for the well-being of every thing and every person involved. It is recognizing the "thouness" in all things, to use Martin Buber's term, even in something we would otherwise see as being an "it." It is recognizing the interiority, the soul, within all things and seeking to unite with and empower the light within that soul. Love is a commitment that you make to that which you wish to manifest (and to the new you that you are manifesting) to act on behalf of its (and your) well-being and highest good.

USING TRANSPERSONAL WILL. In addition, you also may invoke the power of your transpersonal will. This is not quite the same as the willpower you may exercise in your life to make something happen. The transpersonal will does not express through force. It is more like the kind of effortlessness that takes over when you are doing something you love. Rather than doing *it*, it seems to be doing *you*.

A metaphor for this is in running. At first, running is an effort; you may have to use your personal will to keep with it and move through the pain and resistance. However, there comes a time when something else clicks within you, and you are running without effort. There is an inevitability about the running; it seems so natural that no other course is possible.

Transpersonal will empowers your seed image, making it more present. It acts with joy and a sense of naturalness, as if no other course were possible. While personal will often comes with a sense of strain and pressure, transpersonal will is graceful and integrated with the world in which it is acting and with the objective it is seeking to unfold.

There is another difference as well. Personal will is usually activated by a specific event or need. Transpersonal will is the projection of your total life purpose and presence into the arena of life. It emerges from the wholeness of you and acts to integrate the specific purpose of the moment into the incarnational purpose of your whole life.

❧

Exercise:
Projecting the Light of Your Will

Sitting in silence, imagine yourself within your heart, in a place of unconditional lovingness within yourself. See yourself in a pool of golden light. From this pool, streamers of light flow out throughout your body and beyond into your memories, your pattern of relationships, your essence, your soul, and into the heart of unity itself. Now imagine from this pool a golden light moving up through your head into a spot about seven inches above your head, where it spreads out to form another pool. As it does so, it changes into a silvery light that is connected to the pool of love within your heart.

Now imagine before you the presence of the new you that you wish to manifest. From this pool of silvery light above your head, see a beam of light flash out, illumining and irradiating this presence. This presence is filled with flashing points of silver light, like millions of stars, that coalesce into a radiance of will-infused being. Through this silver beam of light, this presence also is connected to the wholeness of love and presence within your heart. Hold the image of the light of your will and purpose, the light of your incarnation, infusing and empowering this presence, integrating it with your soul's intent.

Take a deep breath, and as you inhale slowly, see the image of this presence drawn along the line of light to the pool above your head and then down through your head and into your heart, where it dissolves and spreads out to become one with all parts of your being. Now exhale slowly, and as you do, see this presence of the new you coalescing in the golden pool in your heart, traveling up the line of light through your head and out into the silvery pool above you and from there projected out into your world, like an image from a movie projector. Repeat this slow breath and visualization two more times for a total of three times.

At the end of the third projection, give thanks for the will that integrates your life and fulfills that which is for your highest good. Then release the image and spend a moment or two in simple silence. See yourself reentering your everyday world fully grounded and in balance with your life. Then end your meditation.

ALIGNMENT WITH SERVICE. Aligning your manifestation proj-ect with a larger sense of service to your world is a powerful way of integrating what you are doing with the broader and deeper dimensions of your being as well as with what might be called the soul of the world about you. It draws to you the power of that integration, and it also offers perspective upon what you are seeking to do.

The way of doing this is very simple. You imagine how that which you wish to manifest will better enable you to be of service in your world, and you visualize yourself—the new you you are manifesting—as being of service.

Service in this context *can* mean doing good works, such as feeding the hungry, healing the sick, and participating in the many causes and crusades that fill modern life. It can also mean

filling your environment with attitudes and energies that empower, bring joy, and spread love. Service can be housing the
homeless, but it can also be creating a loving and nurturing
atmosphere in your own home for those who share it with you
or who enter into it. It can mean creating an empowering and
creative environment where you work. Service can also mean
acts of meditation and silence that help to heal the noise of
confusion, fear, hatred, and pain that swirl through our collective psychic environment. Service in this context is any action
consciously connected to the unity of all things that acts as a
bridge between the specific need of any place, person, or situation and the source of unconditional love and healing that
resides in the sacred dimension of life.

What service means for you is for you to decide; how you
serve is up to you, based on your perception of your life and
energy and the needs you see around you. Nevertheless, being
of service in some manner is an important part of the manifestation process and is focused upon in this part of the manifestation ritual.

Exercise:
Acting in Service

Imagine how the success of your manifestation can
help you to give better service in your life. Be as
specific as you can. Then write down any ideas,
thoughts, or images that came to you.

Next, imagine the new you. See yourself acting in
service in some manner. Visualize how this new you
enables an empowering and loving energy to flow
from the essence of your being and its connection to
unity out into the specific conditions of your life.

Hold this visualization as long as you can. Then write down any ideas, thoughts, or images that came to you.

Finally, imagine yourself before a holy presence; this may be a place, a person, or a condition, whatever feels natural and sacred to you. Before this presence, make a commitment to be of service in your world, and offer your manifestation project and the presence of the new you toward this end. Be alert to any images or sensations that arise within you as you make this offering. Feel this holy presence embracing and blessing you as the meditation comes to an end. When you are finished, write down any images, thoughts, or feelings that arose from this visualization.

Holding the seed image of my manifestation in my hands, I breathe deeply, drawing a spiritual energy of love from the heart of the Beloved into my being, where it joins with the energy of my presence. Then I breathe out onto the seed, filling it with this love. As I do so, I realize I can love the object of my manifestation whether I receive it or not. Possession is not a condition for my love. I release my manifestation object to find a rightful place in its world, whether that is with me or not.

I breathe deeply, drawing a spiritual energy of will into my being, where it joins with the transpersonal will of my own presence. I then breathe this will out into the seed of my manifestation. In doing so, I empower it to unfold in its own way, to fulfill its relationship to the world, to me, and to the Beloved, whether or not that results in my manifesting my desire.

Once more, I breathe deeply, drawing a spiritual energy of wisdom into my being, where it joins with the wisdom of my own presence. I breathe this spirit of wisdom into the seed of my manifestation. In so doing, I ask that my manifestation reveal to me how I may be of service in my world, whether it can assist me in that service or not; and I ask that it be of service wherever and however it manifests.

Precipitate the Image

Now is the time to cool your reality down, so to speak, and to begin moving back into your personal reality, carrying with you the blessed and charged seed image of the new you.

Now you want to do things that will concretize the image for you and begin to use it to engage with the material world.

One way to do this is to tell one or more stories about your new you. Storytelling is a powerful tool. Instead of just picturing my objective, I tell myself a story about it. In the story, I am my new self, participating in the world in which my manifestation has come to pass. Through the story, I can feel more deeply and sensually just what my new reality will be like. I am fleshing out my seed image, giving it more substance. This gives me a dynamic, even dramatic image that can involve me emotionally as a participant, not just a static picture that I look upon as an observer.

Exercise:
Telling a Story

Think of a story that makes you actively involved with your manifestation. For example, if you are seeking to manifest a new house, see yourself living in it, decorating it, furnishing it, having people over to visit in it. If it is a relationship with a person, see yourself in that relationship, enjoying things together, having conversations, going places, and so forth. Your story should also tell how the manifestation comes about, how it affects others around you, and any other details that make it come alive for you. Feel free to make the story as dramatic and involving as you wish, but keep it realistic. The power of your presence is best invoked by how naturally the seed image fits into your life. A key to manifestation through storytelling is not simply to make a story vivid but to make it *natural* and realistic.

Don't think of your story as necessarily predictive of how your manifestation will come about (though it might be). It is simply an imaginative exercise to give you a deeper sense of attunement. Approach your story in a spirit of fun and adventure, and see what emerges. You may even find clues and insights that can help actualize your manifestation reveal themselves, much like the unfoldment of a dream.

Exercise:
Color and Sound

Akin to storytelling is the use of art to engage you more fully and deeply with your manifestation. It doesn't matter whether you have artistic talent or not. Take some crayons or paints, and make color drawings reflecting your manifestation project and your sense of the new you. See what feelings emerge when you do this. Or make up songs about your manifestation, or poems. No one else need ever see what you do. Use art in any form to stimulate your sense of creative energy.

TALISMAN. You could make a talisman representing your new you. The process is very simple. Take a small object like a stone, a crystal, or a shell—it could be a piece of jewelry—and hold it in your hand. Attune to your presence, and visualize a stream of spiritual force coming down into yourself. Once this energy is centered in you, visualize it flowing out through your hands into the object you are holding. Then attune to your seed image, and experience its felt sense within your self. Make this as clear as you can. Be your new you; inhabit its reality. Then once this is centered and clear in you, breathe the essence of the new you into the object. Lay it by the central candle, asking that it be blessed unconditionally by spirit and by the sacred while you continue with the ritual.

When you come to the end of your ritual, instead of closing the circle normally, step out of your sacred space and allow the object to be alone in the circle with the candle flames. Leave the room for twenty minutes or so. (Make sure, though, that the candles are all burning safely and that you can leave them unattended without danger!) Then return, close the circle as described below, and retrieve your talismanic object.

Wearing or carrying the talisman is a way of providing a point of contact for you with your work in the ritual and with the spirit of the new you. It is as much a memory device as anything, reminding you when you see it or touch it to give thanks to the powers that be for whatever forces are at work to bring your manifestation to a successful conclusion.

Close Sacred Space

When you feel you have brought your seed image back to earth, so to speak, it is time to close the circle. Make sure, however, that you hold in your mind and body a felt sense of the reality and life of your new you. Although you are closing the circle and leaving sacred space, you are not quite finished with the ritual process itself.

You close the circle giving thanks for all you have experienced and received. Then blow out the four candles, acknowledging as you do the spirit of the four directions as manifestations of the physical expression of the sacred. Ask that that spirit flow out into the world, carrying the blessings of the sacred to the four corners of the earth. Finally, blow out the central candle, again giving thanks and offering your manifestation project unconditionally to the sacred.

Inhabit Your New Self

Now you want to take some action that you can do holding the felt sense of your seed image. You want to act as if you are your new you in order to begin anchoring that experience into the physical world.

You could, for example, wash the dishes or clean the garage. You could go to your job and work in the spirit of the new you.

One exercise I have found helpful is to take a "manifestation walk." I like to walk and have found it an effective way to ground the energy of the seed image.

The technique is very simple. Imagine that you are the new you that you wish to manifest, and go for a walk. Be that presence while walking. Feel the sensation of walking, the play of your muscles, the energy in your body, and link that sensation with the presence you are manifesting. You could even imagine that you are physically walking into the new world that will result when the manifestation comes about; imagine that each step you take carries you into your manifestation.

You can embody the energy of the new you during other daily activities. The idea is to *be* the presence of the new you doing that action. Draw on the sensation and physicality of your body in action to give substance and reality to the felt sense of the new you.

In our house, we have a family altar. It is not a place of worship as much as a place where we put objects that are spiritually important to us. When we are manifesting something, I often put something on the altar that represents my manifestation project. An example might be a talisman created during the manifestation ritual as I described earlier, but it could be anything that reminds me and attunes me either to my own presence or to the object of my manifestation. This could also include artwork.

One thing important to me, though, is to approach such an altar in a playful spirit. You are not worshipping your manifestation, but you can certainly play with various ways to enhance its physical reality for you.

MANIFESTATION RITUAL

For your reference, here is an outline of the manifestation ritual I described.

SACRED SPACE
Do something or use something that sets the time and place of this ritual off from the rest of the day as something special. I use a candle and an invocation.

INVOCATION
Activate your sacred space, and invite into it the presence of those sacred forces that are important to you, asking them to consecrate this space for your highest good and the highest good of your project.

SILENCE
Invoke the creative power that emerges from silence and inner calm.

EMBRACE CURRENT REALITY
Make an acknowledgment and an acceptance of your present reality part of the circle, without denial or rejection.

ATTUNE TO COINCIDENCE AND MIRACLE
Get in touch with the creative, stimulating, inspiring energy of wonderment and magic as revealed through the little miracles that can fill our lives.

Attune to Spirit and the Sacred

Using whatever method or tradition is meaningful to you, attune to the sacred and to the transpersonal realms of spirit.

Engage in Blessing

Become part of the higher dimensions of spirit by joining them in giving blessing to the world.

Invoke Presence and Boil Reality

Invoke the playful, creative presence of your holistic self, and focus its energy upon your current reality to quicken it and attune it to new possibilities.

Energize the Seed of the New You

Draw on the power of your spiritual dimension and the spiritual dimension of the world, focusing that power into the seed image of your manifestation and aligning it with your transpersonal love and will.

Precipitate the Image

Use art, storytelling, and other means to ground the heightened energy of your seed image back into your life in ways that enhance its everyday reality for you.

Close Sacred Space

Release the energy of the ritual into your manifestation project and out into the world. Give thanks.

Inhabit Your New Self

Take some physical actions, such as walking or performing a task, while experiencing a felt sense of the reality of your new you. Act as if you are that new you already.

Chapter Nine

Connecting the New You

Once you have taken on and are inhabiting the energy field of the new reality you are manifesting—the body of the new you —the next step is to connect it with the larger reality around you. You are introducing it to your world, so to speak, and seeing what there is and whom there may be that can support your manifestation even while you are inhabiting it from the inside.

Creating a Supportive Context

You can connect your manifestation project by creating a supportive context. You do this by marshaling your resources, confronting your challenges, and connecting with people who can help and empower you.

Knowing your resources is a vital step in beginning any project. In manifestation, your resources include your current physical and financial reality. If you were to simply purchase or use normal transactional means to acquire what you want, would you be able to do so? If you could, that doesn't mean you should not try to manifest it, but it does mean that you begin from a different set of circumstances from someone who has no financial resources to draw on.

Finances are only part of our resources when it comes to manifestation, however. Just as important are inner resources such as creativity and faith. Also, the connections that we have with people—family, friends, co-workers—can be very useful. However magical manifestation sometimes seems, the inner art needs to find and use some routes into your life in order to deliver. So, for example, if you are looking to manifest a new job, knowing some people in the field where you would like to work or putting the word out amongst friends and associates can provide channels for information and contacts to manifest for you. Friends, too, can be sources of insight, encouragement, wisdom, and support; they can empower you and energize you with their faith in your process.

Your own life experiences, the wisdom you've gained, the knowledge you have can be an important resource. You may not wish to be bound by them; the inner art may invite you to take risks or actions that seem illogical to the mind. Nevertheless, applying your innate wisdom to your manifestation project can certainly shape or determine a step that you should take.

❧

EXERCISE:
MAPPING YOUR RESOURCES

I suggest that you take a sheet of paper and draw a small circle in the middle of it. In that circle write down what it is you wish to manifest. Then draw a much larger circle around it and divide that circle into sections, like pie-shaped wedges. Label each section with an area of potential resource. Labels could include finances, friends, contacts, past experience, mental and emotional condition, spiritual practice, health, and any other categories you feel would be important or would have a bearing on what you wish to manifest. Then in each segment, write down just what you think your resources, strengths, and sources of energy and power are in that area. You may surprise yourself by realizing just how truly wealthy you are in ways beyond what a bank account can measure.

Next, after you have this outline of resources, write down what each resource adds to your life. For example, "The money I have helps me pay bills that otherwise would go unpaid," or "My finances give me a sense of security." If the resource is a job, it may give you a sense of accomplishment; friends give you support and companionship. A talent gives you enjoyment, a skill gives you pride and dignity. Whatever gifts and benefits derive from your resources, acknowledge them and write them down. They are sources of empowerment and inspiration, and they represent blessings already present in your life.

Finally, for each resource you have listed, write down how it connects with the objective of your manifestation project. What, if anything, does it have to offer?

∂℗

You may use some or none of these resources in pursuing a particular manifestation project. Synchronicity may happen with no apparent effort or involvement on your part, other than working mentally or imaginatively with the techniques of manifestation. Or the synchronicity—the manifestation—may simply point you in a direction, give you a clue or a boost, and leave you to do the rest yourself, drawing on abilities, contacts, and resources you already have. In fact, this is generally how manifestation works for me: opening the doors of opportunity that I might not have seen or known how to open otherwise. It is then up to me to step through and use my talents in whatever way that opportunity demands.

The important point is that manifestation is not turning over an outcome to some agency outside yourself or becoming dependent on some magical process. This is a disempowering image. Manifestation is always participatory and co-creative. Therefore you cannot ignore or deny the resources you can bring to that process, nor the accountability that naturally results.

Tapping the Power of Change

All manifestation requires some change. It may be something as minor as clearing off garage space for a new car or as major as moving to a new location for a new job. It can mean simply a physical change, or it can require changes of attitudes and behavior, as might be the case if you are manifesting a new relationship. One way to inhabit your manifestation through action is to begin making some of these changes in advance.

I once talked with a young woman who came to me for counseling with the enviable complaint that she was so happy, she thought something might be wrong with her! She was particularly happy in her marriage. When I asked her how she had met her husband, she told me a wonderful story of manifestation. She said that she decided one day to make a list of all the characteristics and traits her ideal mate would possess. Among other things, she wanted a man who was kind, humorous, romantic, and responsible. She planned on having kids, so she wanted someone who would be a good father. She said that she didn't care if he was handsome, but she did want him to be someone who took pride in his body and in how he presented himself. From this list, she formed an image of the man she wanted to marry. She held this image in her mind every day for months, but nothing happened. She met no one who fit the picture she had created.

Then she realized that if she was looking for her ideal mate, he was probably looking for his. What kind of woman and partner would this man want? In short, who should she be in order to be a complement to her ideal partner? Once she knew what her new self would be like, she began making changes to be that person. She took up a program of physical exercise and sports, for example, to give her more physical vitality. She took a gourmet cooking class to enrich her imagination for preparing romantic meals. She stopped smoking. Because she wanted a mate who would be empathetic to the problems of those less fortunate, she even began doing volunteer work at a shelter for the homeless to ensure that she was empathetic herself.

One important thing she realized, she told me, was that if she did all these things simply as a means to an end, the manifestation wouldn't work. She knew that she had to make these changes for herself, not just to attract a mate. She wanted really to be a new person, not just to adopt a lifestyle for a few months and then drop it once she achieved her aims. She was altering her current reality from the inside out by honoring the authenticity and integrity of the new reality she was creating.

A couple of months after she started this process, she met a man who matched her image exactly and who discovered that she matched the image he had created of the woman he wanted to marry. Within weeks they were husband and wife, and they had been happy ever since.

If I think of manifestation simply as an act of acquisition, one in which I am going to get what I want, never mind anyone else's needs or wants, then the idea of using change as a way of inhabiting a manifestation project doesn't make sense. If I have that perspective, then my attitude might well be, "Why should I change? I like me the way I am!" On the other hand, the inner art operates from a co-incarnational perspective. It requires something from me as well as something from that which I am manifesting.

What is required, and the changes that may result, depend on what I am manifesting, of course. A toaster is not going to ask for much from me besides a space on a kitchen shelf and reasonable care and maintenance. A new spouse or a new employer, on the other hand, is going to ask for a great deal more. You will have already considered, when setting up your manifestation project, just what changes your manifestation may require or what would empower it. Connecting the body of your manifestation with your current reality in a way that allows the former to transform the latter means making those changes as much in advance as you can.

Removing Obstacles

Another action I can take to create a supportive context is to examine and confront forthrightly the challenges in my life that I think might obstruct or block my manifestation.

❧

Exercise:
Facing Difficult Conditions

On a piece of paper, make two lists. Title the one "Outer" and the other "Inner." In the first list, you will put down anything in your everyday world that you think keeps you from the specific thing, person, or condition that you want to manifest. This could be money, contacts, opportunities, geography, physical health, and so forth. Be as specific as possible. Are you unable to gain what you wish because of lack of money? Then write down, "I lack $250," or whatever the amount may be. Do you want to start a new career or go back to school, but you have young children? Then write, "My kids are too young for me to go back to school." Whatever seems to stand between you and your manifestation, write it down as specifically as you can.

Do the same with the second list, labeled "Inner." This list deals with attitudes that might get in the way of your manifestation. Again, be as specific as possible. Do you want to manifest a friend but relationships are difficult for you? Then write down, "My shyness gets in the way of meeting people and making friends," or, "My temper creates a wall between myself and others." Fear might be a limiting emotion in your life, but when looking at a specific manifestation project, say precisely what you are afraid of. For example, you might write down the worst thing you think could happen if the manifestation project failed. Instead of saying, "I am afraid," you would say, "I fear that I will lose my apartment if I cannot manifest $500 for rent this month." The reason for being specific is that there may be ways of dealing with or alleviating a particular fear or other negative attitude apart from the manifestation process. You might not be able to deal with fear as such in your life, but you could deal with the fear of eviction by talking the situation over with your landlord or by seeing what sacrifices you might make in other areas of your life to have the money you need for the rent. By making the fear or other emotion specific and related to a concrete circumstance or consequence, you make it more manageable.

When your two lists are complete, after each obstacle or challenge, write one sentence about some action you can take within your current resources to do something about it. If money is a problem on your "Outer" list, then write one thing you can do to help yourself feel better about it; it might be putting five dollars or even one dollar away in a savings account each week, or it might be tithing one dollar or five dollars to a good cause. If your living environment is a problem, then state one action you can do to make it prettier or lighter or healthier. If you are lacking a job, then state one volunteer action you might do each week that could benefit someone else. If your "Inner" list has revealed an attitudinal problem, then write down an action you can take to change it. For example, if your block is low self-esteem, then write something like, "I am going to do some volunteer work," or, "I am going to finish cleaning up the garage." The best cure I have found for low self-esteem is to do something that will give you a sense of accomplishment, particularly if it helps someone else.

Discipline yourself to do each of these actions that you list. The important thing is that, however small or trivial the response to your challenge might be, it is a seed of positive action. It conveys the important message that you are not totally helpless, that you have a power to contribute and to change. This is especially so if any of the actions you take add to someone else's well-being.

Believing in the art of manifestation and using it should not lead you into denial of difficult conditions around you and in your life. You cannot change the difficulties in your life by ignoring them or pretending they're not there. The inner art consists of beginning where you are with what you have and—paradoxically—with what you don't have. If your bank account, your job opportunities, your health, or your social life seem nonexistent, then that is how it is. That is part of your pattern, part of what makes you you. You cannot use the inner art by starting from a false premise, a "fake you." Denying the challenges you face will make them go away or help you to meet them. Manifestation works with the wholeness of your pattern; to use the inner art successfully, you must work with that wholeness, too. You cannot reject part of yourself or part of your reality and expect to work with wholeness.

However, there is more to your pattern than just the difficulties. You do have resources to draw on, and you do have an inner power that is not limited to your immediate physical, emotional, or social situation. The inner art works with spiritual resources and forces that express within time and space but are not bound by their appearances. Synchronicity is a nonlocal phenomenon, meaning that it supersedes normal, linear, logical chains of cause and effect. Something can happen, patterns can unfold, miracles can occur in your life that nothing in your past, your present, your environment, your bank account, your job situation, or your relationships might prepare you for or prevent from happening. You *are* powerful in your full creative potential, but that power is rooted in an acknowledgment of the reality of what is—both the good and the bad, the resources and the challenges—as well as in the potentiality and inspiration of what might be.

Recruiting Your Team of Allies

Once you have a sense of the actions you can take to support your manifestation, even if those actions may not directly bring the manifestation about, you can then set about creating a team of allies. This team can be as small as one other person or as large as a whole community. Friends who can empathetically add their positive energies, their insights, and their help can be important in giving substance and enhanced potential to what you are trying to do. Even just putting the word out about what you are seeking to manifest can sometimes open the very doors through which that manifestation can come.

One thing you could do is to hold a manifestation party. Everyone who came would do so in the spirit of adding energy to your manifestation. They could come with pictures or symbols representative of that which you wish to manifest; they could participate in a ritual with you or in shared meditation or prayer. They could make up stories celebrating the new you. They could share ideas and suggestions on how the manifestation might come about or how you could inhabit it more successfully. They could simply celebrate you as a creative being, affirming your worthiness and empowering you. You, in turn, could give something to each of those who attend in recognition of the sharing and communal nature—the co-incarnational and co-creative nature—of manifestation itself. The party could be as simple or elaborate as you wish it to be. If you're simply manifesting a toaster, then an all-night bash might be fun but excessive (though who am I to say?); on the other hand, if you are seeking to manifest a new job or find a new relationship, then a lively and supportive manifestation party might be just the ticket!

I can testify to the power of such a collective event. In one group I worked with, we all would support each other in our individual manifestation projects, and on occasion we would have what we called empowerment sessions. During such a session one person would share a project he or she wanted to undertake, and everyone else would provide meaningful support. Such support could take the form of additional ideas, brainstorming, helpful criticism, or offers of material aid. Ridiculing someone's idea or simply dismissing it was not allowed, nor were the participants allowed to substitute their ideas for those of the person being empowered or to shift the conversation to their own needs and desires.

For example, on one occasion, we met to listen to one of the men in the group, Milenko Matanovic, who wanted to create a book. His idea was to produce an anthology of interviews with famous artists, musicians, actors, religious leaders, and others about how their work reflected a spiritual intent or context. He wanted to call the book *Lightworks*. His challenge was that he had never done a book before, and English was not his native language. There was also the problem of contacting the potential interviewees and getting them to agree to take part in this project.

We listened as he outlined his idea and gave a list of the people he wanted to interview. As he went along, I realized there were points he wanted to make that I would do differently if I were doing the project, and I would have selected a different group of subjects. I also had doubts about Milenko's command of the language at that time, and I felt he might be taking on too big a task. However, my role in this situation was not to criticize his idea or stop its flow of energy with my doubts or to tell him how I would do it. I and the others were there as friends of the project, so to speak, and servants of its empowerment. (We had business meetings where doubts, criticisms, and challenges could be voiced!)

A critical element in this empowerment was to realize that we were not supporting a *project* but a *person*. This made it easy to attune to Milenko and to allow my love and respect for him to be the overriding energy and the context within which the work took place. Whereas focusing on the project would have made it easier to slip into a critical and analytical mode, focusing on Milenko meant being sensitive to what was happening for him as a person. For example, I needed to listen past his words to his intent and help him clarify what he wanted and needed to say in order to express his creativity. We were empowering Milenko, not his book, and the end result could have been that he might have found a way of fulfilling his aims other than through this book.

The session lasted about three hours, and by the time it was over, not only did Milenko feel encouraged, but we all felt highly energized. We had also worked out ways to get the interviews, identified allies who might be helpful, and clarified the idea so that we could all see the value this book could have. In fact, after that time Milenko went on not only to get all the interviews he had wanted and to produce a very fine book, but that book led to his writing another based on his own work and teachings, which is called *Meandering Rivers and Square Tomatoes*.

You may wish to have just a single buddy as opposed to a group to share your process with. Having another point of view to bounce off of and a person who can act as a mirror for your process can be extremely helpful. I almost always involve either my wife or a friend in any manifestation project I am undertaking. The addition of one other person's energy is synergetic rather than additive; the result is more than just the sum of your individual perspectives. A whole new and mutually supportive dynamic is created.

Mindfulness

As we go about our daily business, opportunities may arise or clues may appear that can help us with our manifestation. We simply need to be alert to them. This is in addition to the kind of mindfulness required to stay attuned.

For example, I once talked with a man who was trying to manifest a consulting job, without much success. He decided to fly to another city, where he could meet some prospective clients. As it turned out, none of them were in the market for his services, but on the return plane trip, he got into a conversation with a man sitting next to him. It turned out that this second gentleman was a businessman who needed exactly the kind of consulting the first man had to offer. From this conversation, the consulting job he wanted manifested, and when it turned out successfully, it led to other jobs and clients until he had a thriving business. Meeting the man on the plane was not something he could have planned on, but he had taken steps to develop his ideas and his marketing plan, he knew what he could offer, and he was on the road interviewing potential clients. He did not stay home waiting for the job to drop into his lap. He was taking action and therefore creating a supportive context for his manifestation. At the same time, he was open to unexpected opportunities. He was being mindful.

In my experience, it often works out that what you will manifest is opportunities to fulfill your desire rather than the thing, person, or condition itself. If so, then you must be prepared to act positively and in a committed fashion upon those opportunities. The opportunity may even come as an intuition that requires attention and perhaps immediate action.

Paying attention to your intuition or hunches can lead to the manifestation you wish or at least to a step toward it. Having worked as a game designer, I like to keep in touch with innovative game designs as they come on the market. I recently heard of a new game that used cards in a special way, and I wanted to get a copy to study while on a trip. None of the game stores in Seattle carried it, though, and when I called the company directly, they said the game would not be available for another two weeks. The very next day, I was driving home from a class I was teaching in Seattle when I had a strong intuition I should visit a particular hobby store. To do so meant a detour of some twelve miles or more through the city, but I decided to follow my intuition. When I arrived at the store and walked in, there on a shelf right in front of me was the game I was looking for. It had arrived in the store that morning, two days before I was to leave on my trip.

There is another set of opportunities to which you can be alert in addition to those that further your own manifestation project. These are opportunities to practice manifestation on behalf of someone else. Most manifestations come about through some form of human agency: Someone does something for someone else. One way to inhabit and energize the body of your manifestation is to be a source of manifestation for another person or to be a link in a chain of events that leads to that other's manifestation. As I pointed out in Chapter 5, acts of giving, tithing, and charity enhance your participation in your community and open you to the presence of a larger wholeness. Such giving is not a means to an end. It is an act of connection and co-incarnation that is complete in itself. It lifts you beyond the gravity well of your personal concerns and opens you to larger vistas and sources of energy. It allows your new you to take its place as a worthy member of your expanding reality.

Chapter Ten

Manifestation Never Fails, But . . .

You know your manifestation project is complete when you receive what you wanted. It will come either in the form you specified or in some equivalent way, in which the essential intent of your seed image is fulfilled even if the form is different from what you expected. The question is, how long should you wait for this to happen?

How Long?

The simple answer is, for as long as it takes. You have no way of knowing how a synchronistic event that can fulfill your manifestation will take place or what process is involved in bringing all the necessary elements together to enable it to happen. I have had manifestations occur within minutes of setting the process into motion. At other times they have taken years.

You may set a deadline as part of the process itself. You may need the object of your manifestation within a certain time period. Simply make that timeline part of the image and identity that you create. The deadline becomes then one of the parameters by means of which you will know if your manifestation succeeds or not (at least in the way you wanted).

On the whole, however, I prefer to work without imposing deadlines. I prefer to keep the energy of urgency out of my inhabiting process. Even if I do have a practical deadline, I have found that urgency or anxiety can diffuse my attention and concentration. It can disrupt the steadiness of the energy I am putting into the process.

Even without a deadline, though, is there a time when you should call it quits and go back to the drawing board? Well, that depends on you and on what you are manifesting. If it is something that can wait, then I would simply wait, checking in on the process every now and again. On the other hand, if the situation has changed and you simply want to abort the project, you can do that at any time. I depend a lot on my intuition for such things. If when I check in on my project, it seems to have little life to it, I cannot drum up much enthusiasm for it, or it does not feel centered and vital in my body, then chances are the energy has dissipated or run into some obstacle. Then it is time to end it.

Ending a manifestation project before you have received what you wanted is very simple. When you check in by entering your imaginal space and attuning to the process, visualize the image of the new you—the seed image of your manifestation—as you have been doing, but now see it unravel, dissipate, and dissolve. Draw its creative energy back into your self, giving thanks for any blessings it carries and for any help you have received or invoked as part of the process. Then let go of any attachments or connections you have formed with the object of your manifestation (this is particularly important if you have focused it upon a person or a group of people), proclaiming that this particular manifestation is now finished. You may add any flourishes to this procedure that you wish. The idea is consciously and deliberately to dispel the image and matrix you were working with and to reclaim its energy, releasing any and all attachments you may have developed.

In determining how long you should allow a manifestation to proceed, try to avoid impatience. In the growth of any organism (and the new you that you are manifesting is like an organism), there are periods of rapid and energetic activity and growth and periods of quiescence and consolidation. Creation often proceeds in a sporadic rhythm, and long periods can be spent on a plateau in between growth spurts. You want to allow for these plateaus, these quiet periods, and not give up too soon.

By the same token, calling it quits when a project doesn't seem to be going anywhere and you cannot feel any energy in it creates an open space for something new to appear. It allows you to evaluate what has happened and learn from it. Sometimes going back to the drawing board is precisely the most creative thing that you can do. Don't be afraid to let the process go, but don't kill it out of impatience either. The inner art rewards those who can learn through practice to be sensitive to the rhythms and pulses of incarnation.

Manifestation Never Fails!

There are at least five ways in which a specific act of manifestation can be resolved.

First, we can receive what we asked for. We would call such a manifestation a success. (We might receive even more than we asked for, in which case it's a smashing success!)

Second, something manifests that brings us the pattern or energy or essence of what we wished but not in the form we wanted. Unless we are sensitive to the levels deeper than form, we might not recognize what actually came as a successful manifestation. We might account it a failure, not realizing that in fact our manifestation request has been answered better than we could have hoped. This is why taking time to attune to the pattern and quality of the object of our manifestation is important. Then we can recognize when this quality or pattern is in fact entering our lives, even though the specific form we had imagined is not.

A third possibility is that the form we imagined manifests, but somehow the essence or pattern is not quite there. Here the impulse is to accept what has come, but again a sensitivity to the deeper levels of pattern, quality, and essence can be important. What has manifested may be good, but it is not the best; as Peter Caddy often said in the early days of Findhorn, the good is the enemy of the best. In effect, this third result represents an incomplete manifestation; what has appeared may be only the shadow of what is still forming and precipitating into our lives.

As an example, some years ago my wife and I felt we needed a new house. We made this our manifestation project, and we had a fairly good idea of what we were looking for. A friend called up to say that a house had come on the market that seemed exactly what we wanted. It was large enough for our family, and it had two attached outbuildings that were already set up as offices—the answer to my dream of a separate writing space and library. The place was relatively secluded, had an extra acre of land—and even a tree house, which thrilled my kids. It seemed that everything we had specified at a form level was there—yet somehow the inner essence we were looking for was not. Something was not quite right. The form was present, the soul was not. If we had not been sensitive to that essence, it would have been very tempting to say yes, but we said no instead.

As a matter of fact, upon reflection, we came to the conclusion that we really didn't need a new house. We realized we had not explored all the possibilities of the house we were in and that there were creative and fun things we could do there to meet our needs.

To know when to say no to a manifestation is as important as knowing when to say yes.

The fourth result is when a period of time has passed and nothing seems to be happening. Then, as I have suggested, we may decide to put the whole project onto a back burner, turning our attention and creativity in other directions. The manifestation process is not finished, but now we must let it alone to find its own timing. We release it and move on to something else.

Finally, there are cases when nothing manifests, at least as far as we can tell. We may have waited a respectable time, done our attunements, held our vision, done everything we could, and still nothing. Why, and what do we do about it?

The first thing to realize is this: *Manifestation never fails.* It only takes a different form from what we expected.

This may seem like a semantic cop-out, but it is true nonetheless. Of course, the truth of it depends on how we view manifestation. If all we're seeking is the acquisition of some particular thing, then such acquisition can fail; if that's where our mind is, then we miss the deeper levels where failure is simply success in a different guise.

I understand this best in terms of science. When I worked as a researcher in college, there were times when an experiment did not do what I expected; every such failure, however, contained information that helped me run another experiment that would do what I expected. In science, a negative result can be as useful (if not as desirable) as a positive result, since both provide important information. In a universe made up of information, that's not to be sneezed at!

Every act of manifestation, however it turns out, involves learning. We learn a new pattern. We learn something about ourselves. We learn something about our world. In some manner we are changed by engaging with our inner art. New and important insights can develop, and we may be in a better position for manifesting than we were earlier.

Knowing that I have learned something is not always a comfort when what I really wanted was a new car or a different job. Nevertheless, if I adopt the attitude that I have failed, then I may overlook the valuable lessons and information that I have gained in the process. I can accept that the manifestation did not work in this instance and still benefit from having practiced the inner art. The next time, it will be easier and I will do better.

But If It Does . . .

Here are some reasons why manifestation doesn't work in the way we think it should and some suggestions as to what you might do about it.

IS MY MANIFESTATION TOO INCONGRUOUS?

It may be that your manifestation has too few connections with who you are or with your current reality. You manifest what you are, and what you are is in a pattern of interrelationship and mutual definition with your immediate world. If that which you wish to manifest is incongruent or incompatible with your character, your habits, your values, or your way of living, it is inauthentic to you. It cannot naturally draw on the energy of your life, your patterns, or your essence to fuel its manifestation. More often than not, like does not attract unlike. There must be either complementariness or similarity. What you need to do is increase the congruency between yourself and that which you wish to manifest.

This problem of incongruence can arise from lack of meaningful and realistic information about what you wish to manifest or about yourself. This results in faulty connections or no connection at all with the essence and identity of what you are manifesting. Without that attunement that honors the reality on both sides of the process, you are engaging in wishful thinking, not manifestation.

To deal with this issue, step back and reevaluate. Check for congruency. This may well mean looking more deeply into the levels of essence and pattern belonging both to you and to your objective. Get more information about the reality of what you wish to manifest, as well as its relationship to collective reality and to your personal condition. Then, if you still want it, you must make changes in your own life in order to increase your compatibility with your goal.

The incongruity may be with the scope of what you are trying to manifest. It is almost a cliché in teachings on manifestation to say that you can have it all, that there are no limits upon you. I would phrase that differently. I would say that you should not diminish your creative potential, but all creativity works through boundaries and limits in order to produce something specific. You do have limits. Without them you lack definition and focus. To write this book, I must choose not to do other things that might be equally or even more enjoyable in the moment. If I try to do several things at once, they all may suffer from the lack of my creative focus. Every choice I make—every yes—is a no to something else.

The fact is, you cannot have it all at any given moment. You can only really have just what you can integrate and use; everything else becomes surplus and waste and potentially burdensome, even dangerous.

If the improbability of your goal is because you are trying to do too much or be too much all at once, so that it is incongruous with your current capabilities, limitations, talents, skills, or life situation, then break it down into smaller components if possible. Tackle these smaller bits. Choose intermediate goals that are specific, measurable, achievable, and compatible with who you are and where you are starting from. If you are a political unknown with no administrative experience, don't try to become President of the United States right off; run for the school board as a first step! Or better still, serve as an assistant to someone on the school board to learn the ropes.

Congruency is involved with collective reality as well as with your individual personal reality. This collective reality includes both cultural expectations and worldviews and the images and expectations of those around you. What you wish to manifest may be incongruous with either of these or both.

For example, until recently in the United States, an African-American or a woman would have faced daunting odds to be elected President. The chances of succeeding in such a manifestation would have been highly improbable. Likewise, if you wish to create a new career for yourself, especially one that would force people to see you in a new way, the expectations of friends and family may be incongruous with your new identity and purpose. They may consciously or unconsciously resist the changes you wish to make, because it means they, too, must change.

This does not mean you cannot change that collective reality; after all, that is exactly what many pioneers, explorers, and inventors do. Columbus inhabited a collective cultural reality that said the earth was flat, but he transformed that cultural perception. Likewise, I knew a man who went from being a successful businessman to being a painter, completely altering his lifestyle but having to deal with and overcome the fears and expectations of his family and friends in the process.

Collective reality is not necessarily an obstacle, but it is a factor in our manifestations; if that collective reality is opposed to your manifestation, it doesn't mean that you cannot succeed. You do, however, have to incorporate enough energy and thoughtfulness in your process to diminish that incongruity, or you need to reconsider what you are manifesting.

To deal with incongruity with collective reality, you must explore your own attachments to that reality. You must examine the extent to which you draw your validation, your sense of well-being, even your identity from what others think or what your culture expects. How dependent are you on the perspectives of others? Can you sufficiently separate yourself from the ocean of collective thoughts and images around you to navigate through its currents and find a new way? How confidently and fully can you manifest something that is different from what is expected of you?

Remember, you do not wish to deny the collective reality or act as if it weren't an issue. That can lead to wishful thinking. You want to acknowledge it and deal with it appropriately while still hewing to your own vision. Though the collective reality may be in conflict with your manifestation project, you also should not internalize that conflict. Becoming adversarial only dissipates the energy of the manifestation by diverting your attention and your passion and can block you from receiving messages and insights from the collective reality around you that can be helpful (if only by pointing out possible pitfalls).

HAVE I GIVEN MY MANIFESTATION TOO LITTLE ENERGY?

All manifestation requires energy of some nature to give vitality and momentum to the inner and outer repatterning that it represents. In the language of physics, if you think of a manifestation as a discontinuity (a quantum leap) between two patterns (premanifestation and postmanifestation), then a packet of energy is required to shift between the two. This may be physical energy, such as may be involved in the form of physical work, attentiveness, or general vitality. It is more likely energy of an emotional nature (such as desire or enthusiasm), of a mental nature (the clarity of the holistic image), of a spiritual nature (the degree of release, serenity, and poised alertness, or the degree of attunement and alignment), or a combination of all the above. The energy you have available to give to your manifestation may also be tied to your deeper willingness for the manifestation to take place, a factor I discuss further on.

The greatest drain on the energy available to you to manifest may be that you are not living sufficiently in the present. You may be identifying yourself not as a vital creative individual engaging with life in the moment but as someone in your past. Your energy goes into the past to keep alive images of past wounding, hurts, problems, failures, and calamities.

We talked about this as part of the manifestation fitness program. As I said then, the best solution I know of for this kind of energy loss is loving forgiveness of all that has happened to you in your past. Forgiveness is not admitting that your wounding was all right or that justice should not be done. Rather, it is forgoing or giving over the images of your pain so that your energy can return to you in the present. After all, you are not manifesting in the past; you are doing so right now.

There may be other reasons why you are not giving enough energy to your manifestation. Check out your manifestation fitness program. You may simply be tired or in ill health. Take a vacation from it all. Refresh and re-energize yourself, then go back to your project. Treat your project as a game or as play; approach it as you would a sport or activity that you enjoy and are excited about. You should especially be on the lookout for enervating attitudes such as discouragement, depression, self-pity, or self-disparagement. Self-esteem is important to maintaining good energy levels, as are the simple ordinary things that help people feel vital, such as diet, rest, exercise, and activities that build your physical well-being and morale.

Is my timing off?

Remember that manifestation is a co-creative phenomenon. Others are involved in one way or another. Their reality, their timing, can affect the speed with which a manifestation happens. I may feel a strong intuition to send you some money (which you are trying to manifest), but I may need to wait until some other action takes place, like selling some stock or completing a sale, before I have the money to send. If timing is the problem, then the thing to do is to have patience.

Am I truly open to the changes required by my manifestation?

All manifestation represents a change of some degree in your life. It is the unfoldment of a new pattern. Some part of you may not be willing for that change to take place and may be withholding energy from the process. To see if this is a problem, perform some additional self-inventory. Get in touch with your pattern and essence. Look again at what will change if the manifestation takes place. Are you clinging to something that might change, unwilling to let it happen? Can you address that resistance, understand it, and let it go? Or should you pay attention to its warning? Remember that the resistance might not be bad or wrong. Perhaps it is telling you something about yourself and your situation that may lead you to change your objective. Whatever the reason, with deeper understanding you can try again or change the direction and goal of your manifestation.

Is my objective clear and specific enough, or is it too specific?

Perhaps the attunement and alignment you have made with the object of your manifestation is incomplete. You don't really have a clear sense of what you are trying to manifest. Perhaps you are trying to deal with a symptomatic need or desire rather than with something fundamental. For example, you want to manifest a car to commute to your job, but what you really need and want is a different job, one that is closer to home. What is the real need that you are trying to meet? Ask yourself how that need might otherwise be filled. Or ask other people to help you think into and attune to your object of manifestation and its relationship to you. They may see patterns and connections that you are missing.

On the other hand, perhaps you are being too specific and too particular about what you wish, narrowing the conditions under which it can come to you. It may be time to pull back and give life some elbow room to work on your behalf, even if the form of the outcome is different from what you specified. Your manifestation may be suffering from too much control on your part, interfering with the synchronicity and serendipity of it all.

AM I PAYING ATTENTION TO OPPORTUNITIES AND ALTERNATIVES?

The success of a manifestation project can come to you through opportunities that arise. Sometimes these opportunities may have no obvious relationship with what you are trying to manifest but can lead to other connections that do. I have often had this experience. My going to Findhorn in the first place was an example of this. I knew I wanted to manifest a new cycle of work, but I was not anticipating it starting in Scotland! I thought my trip to Findhorn was just a vacation sidelight en route to what I was looking for.

Also, alternative forms of your manifestation objective may present themselves to you. The question you must ask is how open you are to recognizing these alternatives or opportunities when they appear. After much practice of staying alert and in present time, I have learned that when such an opportunity presents itself or such an alternative arises, it carries a distinctive quality, like a metaphysical flavor or odor, that says, "Pay attention right now! This is important." As I discussed earlier, each manifestation project has its own unique inner signature. Part of the practice of inhabiting is to listen inwardly for it.

Be alert! Be sensitive to what is happening around you. Use your intuition, your body sensing, your feelings, and your intelligence to keep attuned to your world. You may find you have been close to the fulfillment of your manifestation and not recognized it yet.

WHAT AM I GIVING AWAY OR CREATING IN MY LIFE?

Your manifestation may be blocked because your energy is too focused upon yourself or bound up in your own needs. Manifestation is fueled by a process analogous to respiration, a rhythm between outbreath and inbreath. It builds on the quality of your energy exchange with the world around you. If you are only breathing in—taking but not giving—there comes a time when you can take no more. Your energy is blocked.

Ironically, though we start a manifestation project out of a sense of need, a feeling of neediness can block it. Metaphorically, the gravity pull of our need—which is really the pull of our fear—is so strong that the energetic impulse of our manifestation cannot escape it; it is like a spaceship that cannot break free of the earth's gravity.

Perhaps there is no room, either literally or figuratively, in your life for what you want until you give something else away. Manifestation is about incarnation, not acquisition, and incarnation demands balance. You cannot limitlessly acquire without becoming buried under the energy and attachment of your acquisitions.

If you suspect this is the case (and be honest with yourself!), then see what you can do to unblock yourself. Give something away that you no longer need but that you've been hanging on to. Look for ways you can be a manifestor for someone else. Discover what service you might render in your community. Explore something you can do that is creative. Don't focus on your need, but affirm your identity as a creator of wealth, a source of energy; then do things that express and support that identity. Remember, wealth is measured not in money but in the increase of possibility, energy, potential, empowerment, and creativity in your world. Ask yourself what doors you can open for others. What potential can you unlock? What empowerment can you offer? How can you increase the vitality and openness of your life situation?

Exploring ways that you can give yourself to your environment may be just the ticket for unblocking yourself and getting your energy flowing again. It is the ticket for once more standing in the stream of life that turns the mill of manifestation.

Am I being protected from my own desires by a higher power?

There is a final reason why your manifestation may not be working. I call it protection. The inner art presupposes consciousness and intelligence acting within the domains of pattern, of essence, and of unity. Such levels of awareness may go unnoticed by our everyday, personality-oriented, matter-oriented consciousness unless we have undertaken some form of spiritual and psychological practice that opens us to them. These more embracing and holistic domains of consciousness go by many names: soul, spirit, the higher self, the holy guardian angel, even the God within. They occupy a spectrum that extends from the personal to the impersonal to the mystery of the sacred itself. Along this spectrum is a range of perception and perspective that is wide and deep and less constricted by ordinary parameters and ideas of space and time.

From this range of awareness comes a more comprehensive vision and wisdom that perceives what you do not: that actually achieving your objective will not work to your highest good in the long (or short) run. Perhaps the manifestation cannot be truly integrated into your life, so it would ultimately be disruptive and distorting to the wholeness of your pattern and its unfoldment. Perhaps it would block a flow of spirit or energy from your essence. Perhaps it would have no effect on you but would harm or impact someone with whom you are connected, creating problems at a co-incarnational level. So whatever the reason, the process is blocked or slowed down.

I do not offer this as an easy, feel-good rationalization. Sometimes we justify things that happen (or don't happen) to us by saying that they were for our highest good. If we can learn from the situation and gain wisdom from it, then that may have been correct, or at least we can make it so. There are certainly times when we are protected from our own rashness. But to say that every situation, whatever the outcome, is for our highest good is to lose the power to discern and to discriminate. Such a one-dimensional response disempowers us. We have an obligation, I believe, to think and intuit into a situation with all the faculties at our command to see just what it means for us. There may be warnings involved. There may be genuine error or failure on our part. Saying that everything is okay can blind us to important information that we need if we are to grow in wisdom and capability, honing our skills of incarnation and co-creativity.

So the reason why a manifestation is not working may have nothing to do with our "highest good" or with the protective intervention of a higher power. On the other hand, it may. This is where the practice of spiritual work is important, so that you can learn to see more deeply into a situation or process and see if some other level of being is in fact intervening on your behalf.

If you feel this is the case, then give thanks, and ask for clarification and insight. Do your best to attune to the situation, using prayer, meditation, intuitive tools such as Tarot or the I Ching or whatever method is in harmony with your spiritual path. The manifestation project then becomes a means for spiritual growth and a deepening of your sensitivity to the spiritual dimensions of life. In this manner it augments the power of a regular spiritual practice to expand your everyday awareness into those extended ranges of consciousness that we call the spirit. Then you learn to see more profoundly and clearly for yourself the patterns and processes that make up your life and discover a growing attunement with the sacred mystery and love at the heart of life.

Whatever its results, each manifestation project adds to your information about yourself, enhances your awareness, and thus enriches the patterns and connections you form with life. Sometimes an act of manifestation, even one that does not produce what you wanted or expected, is really a step toward a greater reality already taking shape in your life. After all, your whole incarnation is one great act of manifestation; all the little manifestations you perform are the petals of its unfold-ment.

Whatever its results, do not fail to be grateful to the process and grateful to all those, known and unknown, who partici-pated in it. Be grateful to life, grateful to the sacred, and grate-ful to your own self.

Gratefulness completes the co-creative cycle and opens us to the cosmos; it opens us to wonder and to grace. It is liberating and energizing. Even if the manifestation did not work out, you can still be grateful for whatever you have learned. There will be further opportunities to manifest, to grow, to learn, to earn, to create, and to co-create.

Chapter Eleven

Beyond the Inner Art

When I began teaching classes on manifestation, I considered it a sidelight to my main interest, which was (and still is) the nature of spirituality and spiritual practice. What has always concerned me in my career as a teacher and writer is the blend of the ordinary and the sacred or the spirituality of everyday life. A guiding question for me is how the ordinary routines of our day can become portals into a larger cosmos and into our deepest spirit.

At the same time, I have recognized the many ways in which our understanding of creation has changed in this century and continues to change. While these changes do not render the essence of traditional spiritual teachings and practices passé, they do suggest that we find new images in which to express it. When quantum mechanics, chaos theory, systems theory, and ecology become primary sources for metaphor and behavior in our culture, we need to see ourselves and the things around us in some new lights. So I have also sought to understand what a holistic, systemic, ecological, planetary spirituality might be like. In what ways would it continue the ancient traditions, and how would it differ and demand new insights and ways of expression?

Both of these questions—the nature of an everyday spirituality and the nature of an emerging holistic and global spirituality —continue to guide my work, and they will undoubtedly do so for the remainder of my life. They are not the kinds of questions that can be answered in any final way; nor should they be. Some of the answers lie in the journey itself and in the explorations it entails.

However, when I was asked by a local church to give a talk on manifestation some years ago, which was followed by other talks and then by classes, I realized that in the study of manifestation was a chance to bring these two explorations together. After all, manifestation arises from desire, which is as ordinary a phenomenon as one is likely to find; furthermore, how we manifest is influenced by how we view ourselves and our world. What would manifestation be like, I wondered, if I explored it through the lens of an emerging worldview based on systems thinking, ecology, and quantum dynamics? This book grew out of that question.

Part of my intent is to honor our needs, wants, and desires. Not all of them are necessarily of equal value or good for us or representative of our wholeness. Some desires arise from and perpetuate simple selfishness and self-gratification. Others arise from a deeper sense of our participation in and our responsibility to the world around us. However, in our everyday world we are not going to stop desiring. Desire is a natural human impulse.

What I set out to find was something like an "aikido of desire." I wanted a way to use the energy of my desires to take me to a deeper part of my own being that was in touch with the holistic or spiritual side of the world's being. I wanted a technique that would generate a creative energy and also enable me to penetrate into the soul's domain. I wanted to develop a holistic practice of incarnation—which I sometimes call a spirituality of incarnation. For it has always been clear to me that when we manifest, we are actually crafting our lives.

Rather than deny desire or imply that we should not have wants and needs, I have opted for a technique in which our desires become potential points of reflection and invocation. As such, this technique can be used even when we don't actually need to manifest what we want, when we can simply buy it or make it or bring it into being in normal transactional ways. Manifestation is a way of using any desire as a starting point for a spiritual journey.

Of course, there is much more to a spiritual practice than manifestation. I am certainly not suggesting that you make it the essence or totality of your spiritual life; that would be a very narrow practice indeed. However, it can be an opportunity, no matter how trivial the desire, to explore connections, patterns, alignments, and the flow of both material and spiritual energy through your life.

When you make manifestation a spiritual practice, then the perspectives it brings overflow into other aspects of your life. You begin naturally seeing yourself and your world in terms of interconnected and co-incarnational patterns. The reality of the community in which we all live becomes more apparent. The vision of your incarnation becomes broader, more ecological, more compassionate. Your attitudes and actions reflect a larger, more complete humanity.

How you use the inner art is up to you. It is your incarnation you are crafting, so you need to find the approach that works for your unique situation. My intent has been to offer both a worldview and some guidelines to help you in this process.

Manifestation as Fencing

When I was in college, I took up fencing. Dueling with swords appealed to the swashbuckler within me, and I was attracted to the blend of mental and physical skill that the sport entailed.

For the first few weeks, I hardly ever lifted a sword. Most of what we did were stretching exercises and wrist movements. Even after I got my sword, nearly every training session involved endless repetitions of the proper wrist movements, the correct stances, lunges, and retreats, and so forth.

My first duels were clumsy affairs. Part of my mind was on my opponent and part was on how to move my wrist to parry, riposte, deflect, how to move my legs, how to crouch. I was very mindful of the techniques. Later, I would sit on the sidelines and watch the advanced students and members of the fencing team have at it, and I would marvel at the smooth and fluid motion of their bodies, arms, wrists, and swords. It seemed like it all flowed into one graceful action.

Manifestation is like that. In the past three chapters, I have been describing techniques and exercises that make up a manifestation project. They are like the wrist exercises I learned in fencing. But like graceful swordplay, this inner art is really a seamless flow of attunement. A manifestation project does not need to be broken down into segments, steps, or phases except to get a feel for what you are doing. Once you have that feel, you will perform your manifestation projects in your own way, usually as a graceful flow of attunement from start to finish. There may be no need for a ritual or a formal practice of any kind, simply an attunement to your world and to that which you wish to manifest and an invocation of your presence.

Peggy, a good friend and one of my manifestation students, tells this story: "I've always had uncanny luck in manifesting real estate. I have story after story—each more serendipitous than the last. I was always the one who would find spaces for any of the organizations with which I was involved in Boston, whether it was office space, retreat center space, or teaching space. I've also seemed to have the same luck in finding personal space. Years ago, I decided that it would be fun to have a house on the ocean during the summer. Boston gets very hot and muggy, and the shoreline north of Boston is cool and incredibly beautiful. I told my husband the idea in the winter but then never acted upon it. Finally at the end of May, much too late to find a good place, I found myself pronouncing one day that we were all going to Gloucester [north of Boston] and we were going to find a great place right on the water. Cheap.

"I had no conviction that we'd find a place, I just said it. So my husband, my son, his friend, and another friend all climbed into the car. The Red Sox were playing on the radio and they were losing the game, so my husband was in a terrible mood. He was also mad that I hadn't looked before and kept saying there was no way we'd find a place.

"We drove around the shore aimlessly while we tried to call a particular Realtor. She wasn't in. Finally as we were driving along the shore one last time, I suddenly told my husband to hang a right. We drove to the end of a road, and there on the hill to the right was a gorgeous summer home, sitting out on the rocks looking over the Atlantic Ocean. 'I wonder how anyone would ever get to rent that place?' I said aloud.

"We took off to go home, and just as we were about to leave Gloucester city limits, I saw a phone booth. I jumped out of the car and called the Realtor one more time. She answered. 'I'm looking for a big house to rent right on the water,' I told her. 'I just got a call on a house where the renter just fell through,' she said. Guess which house it was—right, the very one I had been gazing at."

Manifestation can become a natural flow of your life, allowing you to be intuitively guided to be in the right place at the right time to bring a particular manifestation into being, just as Peggy was. You will be inhabiting your presence more and more fully, and the result will be a growing pattern of synchronicity and blessing in your life.

Paradoxically, you may then discover the need to manifest becoming less and less because the sense of wholeness in your life will be deeply satisfying in its own right and because you will find your needs and desires often being met without your having to set up specific manifestation projects to bring them about. Your whole life and its co-creative interaction with your world will become your manifestation project, and you will find yourself in a flow of giving and receiving that truly expresses the wholeness of your co-incarnational nature. That is when the inner art truly comes alive. That is when it expands from simply being a technique to being a deep attunement to the creative force of life itself.

Experiencing this attunement and being a contributor to the shape of the reality we all experience, a co-creator of our collective cosmos, is the ultimate craft. To shape a reality that honors and reveals our full nature and that, in co-creative alignment with the sacred, empowers and nurtures all of life is the highest calling I can imagine.

It is that calling that is the heart of manifestation. It is the essence of the inner art.

Appendix 1

Manifestation in Groups and Organizations

The inner art can be used by a group as well as by an individual. In fact, manifestation at Findhorn was often conducted as a group process. Over the years I have known and worked with many other organizations that regularly and successfully practice collective manifestation.

The process is the same as for an individual. The objective is to create a seed image of that which the group wishes to manifest, as well as an image of the changes and transformations that may follow for the group as a result of the manifestation; in effect, what will the new postmanifestation self of the group be like? There is the same need to cultivate a positive presence within the group and a sense of coherence and wholeness about the manifestation project. Finally, the manifestation needs to be inhabited, with appropriate energy raised and sustained for this purpose.

There are several ways this can be done, largely depending on the size of the group and the nature of the manifestation. When Findhorn had fewer than a dozen members, everyone would gather together for manifestation meditations upon a particular goal. They would discuss the nature of what they wanted to manifest, such as a new greenhouse, and they would ensure that everyone had the same image, so that one person was not manifesting a small greenhouse and someone else a large one.

As Findhorn grew into a community of two hundred people or more, such gatherings became difficult. The whole community was not always able to meet all together for discussion and meditation around a specific manifestation project. Often a manifestation was conducted by the particular department or individuals for whom the manifestation was intended; thus, the gardeners would manifest what was needed for the garden, while the artists would manifest what was needed for the studios. The smaller numbers of people in a given department made coordination of imagery and effort easier. Still, an attempt was always made to inform the entire community of what was taking place and to enlist as much feedback and support as possible.

If the group is too large for everyone to contribute directly to the seed image, then it can function more in the spirit of a supportive manifestation party and as allies to the primary people involved in the manifestation. A particular group within the organization may take charge of the specific manifestation and be responsible for developing and communicating to others the nature of the image that will be used. In the process of creating that image, using deep visualization, they should invite appropriate feedback, insights, and suggestions from the organization as a whole; once the image is formed, then the larger organization acts as a collection of allies whose primary function is to hold a positive energy for the manifestation.

Positive energy within the group or organization is the equivalent of positive beingness within an individual. It is the level of trust and morale within the organization. The existence of good communication and a free exchange of ideas between all levels of the group is an indicator of positive energy. Excitement and enthusiasm about what the group is doing is another. If the organization is a company, positive energy can be fostered through the working conditions, the opportunity for creative expression and advancement for employees, demonstrations of caring and mutual respect between management and employees, and appropriate rewards for accomplishment. Adding to the intangible quality of the job experience through programs for continuing employee education and training, day care and home leave for mothers and fathers with children, and other programs that create a sense of community can also create a positive energy that is empowering to the company as well as to its employees. Personally, I have often fantasized about the use of bards and poets within organizations to bring the arts, celebration, music, and poetry into the corporate or organizational culture as a way of developing a creative collective consciousness.

Likewise, taking on and embodying the seed image can be done in various ways by different people in the organization. If the group is small enough, then everyone can seek to inhabit the sensed reality of the "new self" of the organization and of that which is being manifested. If the organization is larger, then some people can inhabit it physically, some psychologically, and even some spiritually. (At Findhorn, for example, there are small groups of individuals who regularly meet to meditate and pray on behalf of the well-being of the community as a whole and in support of manifesting the answer to particular needs present in the community.) Each person who is involved should find a particular way of inhabiting the company's or group's new vision in a manner that is comfortable and natural as well as empowering to him or to her.

Another approach is to communicate the nature of the manifestation project throughout the organization, sharing the goal that the group wishes to achieve, and painting an image of the results of a successful manifestation to the organization. Then each person can take on that image as his or her own personal manifestation project. In effect, each person is seeking to manifest the new self of the organization. This image could be carried even further if each person asks who he or she will be—the nature of his or her new self—in the new organizational pattern. This can enable each individual to envision and work positively in advance with those personal changes that will result from the organizational change. This can free up or at least clarify any resistance or fear in individuals that might hinder the collective manifestation.

Encouraging each person in the organization to go through the steps of deep visualization and attunement as if the organization's manifestation were his or her own personal manifestation can be a wonderful way of generating insights and ideas; it can definitely enrich the creative process. This assumes that the procedures and means are there for people throughout the group to communicate ideas with each other.

Using deep visualization in a group setting can also be a wonderful way to gain insights into the character of the organization as it is. Exploring the form, pattern, essence, and unity is a way of seeing into the holistic context within which the organization exists and operates; it can reveal interconnections and patterns that might otherwise go unrecognized. Such information can be useful far beyond the needs of a specific manifestation project; it may lead to ways of improving the internal and external systems, procedures, processes, and connections of the organization as it deals with its members or employees and with the larger society and world beyond.

There is one thing to keep in mind, however. The inner art is a practice of incarnation and empowerment. When properly used, it helps an individual be more in touch with his or her wholeness, authenticity, and creativity. As I never fail to repeat, it is not just a means of acquisition. It is a technique of deepening into a systemic and co-creative perspective of oneself and one's world, and of touching sources of inner power that enhance both individuality and group endeavor. Gaining such a perspective within a group has definite consequences for how the individuals of that group see themselves, each other, and their interactions.

The inner art is not antithetical to hierarchical organizations, but it does not work well in a context of dominance and submission. It encourages a level of freedom in which the individual is able to express her or his insights and act on her or his attunements in a responsible and authentic manner. It encourages co-creativity, not automatic obedience.

Working in an organization is itself an ongoing manifestation project, for everyone—all the members or employees—is constantly incarnating and manifesting the organizational identity. They are each inhabiting it. The more empowering and inviting of individual initiative and contribution such inhabiting can be, the more effectively the inner art can be applied in that group context. Obedience to higher authority can be a perfectly appropriate manner of working within a particular project; it is an efficient and focused way of channeling energy and action. But the individual as a source of creative insight and skilled work, and as a co-creator, co-inhabitant, and co-incarnator of the organization, is more than just a function within a hierarchical organizational chart. The question is whether the organization allows room for such larger possibilities: the ability of people to be more and do more than is covered by their job description alone.

The organization that can use both hierarchical and nonhierarchical or network modes of organizing and utilizing the energy of its people, according to what is needed and appropriate for a particular project, is the organization that will be able to tap the power of the inner art most effectively. If it can enhance through its policies and behavior the well-being, happiness, creativity, and positivity of its people, it cannot help but enhance itself as well.

In using the inner art in groups, synergy is the key. A group that possesses synergy manifests what I call an empowerment economy. Such a group recognizes that its primary wealth lies in its individuals and their creativity and productivity, and in its systemic state: the wholeness and vitality of its collective being. In an empowerment economy, emphasis is placed on assisting individuals to function with as much support and wholeness as possible, viewing them not just as bodies to do work but as spiritual, intellectual, and emotional beings as well. Emphasis is also placed on enabling individuals to work together well in ways that encourage free exchange of information and insights. It is an organizational style that favors ongoing learning, networking, team building, and communication across normal boundaries of department and rank.

This brings up some interesting ideas about the way a business might practice the inner art as it seeks to sell its product or service. From this perspective, the product or service, the workers and employees, the management, the working conditions, the "culture" or spirit within the business, and its relationships to its customers and to the community within which it is located cannot be considered as separate, unrelated elements. They are all part of the presence—the wholeness or systemic self—of the business. It is this systemic self, as much as the individual sales force, that encounters the world; it is the energy infused into the product or service as a result of this systemic identity to which the customer may relate. Literally, a product made or a service delivered with love and care has more charisma and energy than one simply churned out in a mindless fashion, and it will more likely be a higher quality product.

Likewise, in an empowerment economy the customer is seen as more than just a consumer. The customer is also a whole being living within a larger context. The company that can relate both to the individuality of the customer and to his or her larger context is the company that has the greatest chance of manifesting its sale.

A company or group that tries to manifest with no regard to its own or its customers' systemic contexts is operating with only part of its potential energy. It is not attempting to be co-creative. A company that is co-creative with its customers manifests an outcome that is empowering to both on many levels. It will develop a loyal base of customers who also become supporters and part of the systemic identity of the company. For the relational web of the company includes more than its employees; it also includes its customers, its suppliers, and anyone else who deals with it. If the thoughts and feelings of all these people are supportive of the company, this creates a wonderful resource of inner power and energy; if on the other hand a company (or any group) through its actions and policies breeds ill-will and discontent amongst those with whom it deals, just the opposite will occur. It will face both inner and outer obstacles to success.

One of my students, a college professor with years of training and experience in marketing and sales, put it this way: "Selling is most effective when used to manifest the growth and development of the client, the salesperson, and all systems between them. The hard-core selling often seen on late-night TV or with used-car salesmen is not selling at all; it's self-serving manipulation." Such manipulation may coerce a sale, but it does not incarnate a holistically successful business; it does not manifest an empowerment economy.

The company or group interested in nourishing the total growth of its organization on all levels should take into account the systemic perspectives of the inner art. Selling in a nonempowering, nonholistic way is like manifesting simply to acquire. It may get a result, but it leaves a larger context unattended to and even weaker in the process. The empowerment economy works for the benefit of everyone and everything involved. It is a reflection of manifestation as an inner art of incarnation.

Bibliography

I have not found any books that directly approach the inner art of manifestation in quite the way I teach it—which is why I have written my own! However, there are many books that are complementary. The following list could easily have been twice or three times as long, but I think these books are good to get you started. I have divided the books into categories to further help you find what you want.

CONTEXT. These books deal with developing new insights and paradigms, the notion of patterns, systems, co-incarnation, creating reality through perception, and so forth.

Achterberg, Jeanne, *Imagery in Healing*, Boston: New Science Library (Shambhala), 1985.

Anderson, Walter Truett, *Reality Isn't What It Used to Be*, San Franciso: Harper & Row, 1991.

Bateson, Gregory, *Mind and Nature: A Necessary Unity*, New York: Bantam, 1980.

———, *A Sacred Unity*, San Francisco: HarperCollins, 1991.

Bolles, Edmund, *A Second Way of Knowing*, Upper Saddle River, N.J.: Prentice Hall, 1991.

Briggs, John P., and Peat, F. David, *The Looking Glass Universe: The Emerging Science of Wholeness*, New York: Simon & Schuster, 1984.

Davies, Paul, *The Cosmic Blueprint: New Discoveries in Nature's Creative Ability to Order the Universe*, New York: Simon & Schuster, 1988.

———, *The Mind of God*, New York: Simon & Schuster, 1992.

Dossey, Larry, *Recovering the Soul*, New York: Bantam, 1989.

———, *Meaning & Medicine*, New York: Bantam, 1991.

———, *Healing Words*, San Francisco: HarperSanFrancisco, 1993.

Elgin, Duane, *Awakening Earth*, New York: William Morrow, 1993.

Friedman, Norman, *Bridging Science and Spirit*, St. Louis: Living Lake Books, 1994.

Hawken, Paul, *The Magic of Findhorn*, New York: Harper & Row, 1975.

Macy, Joanna, *Mutual Causality in Buddhism and General Systems Theory*, New York: SUNY Press, 1991.

Nadler, Gerald, and Hibino, Shozo, *Breakthrough Thinking*, Rocklin: Prima, 1990.

Peat, F. David, *Synchronicity: The Bridge Between Matter and Mind*, New York: Bantam, 1987.

———, *The Philosopher's Stone: Chaos, Synchronicity, and the Hidden Order of the World*, New York: Bantam, 1991.

Riddell, Carol, *The Findhorn Community*, Scotland: Findhorn Press, 1990.

Senge, Peter M., *The Fifth Discipline*, New York: Doubleday, 1990.

Shealy, C. Norman, and Myss, Caroline M., *The Creation of Health*, Walpole: Stillpoint Press, 1988.

Spangler, David, *A Pilgrim in Aquarius: Spirituality and the New Age*, Scotland: Findhorn Press, 1996.

Wheatley, Margaret J., *Leadership and the New Science*, San Francisco: Berrett-Koehler, 1994.

Wolf, Fred Alan, *The Eagle's Quest*, New York: Touchstone/Simon & Schuster, 1991.

Young, Louise B., *The Unfinished Universe*, New York: Simon & Schuster, 1986.

Zohar, Danah, *The Quantum Self: Human Nature and Consciousness Defined by the New Physics*, New York: William Morrow, 1990.

Zohar, Danah, and Marshall, Ian, *The Quantum Society*, London: Bloomsbury, 1993.

FOUNDATION. The art of manifesting something specific is rooted in how we are manifesting our lives all the time: our general or foundational manifestation. There are a great many books out now that deal with some aspect of getting our lives together, becoming creative, healing ourselves, being whole, gaining a vision, and so forth. Here are some good ones. As you can see, I am particularly fond of Marsha Sinetar's books. They all deal eloquently with helping us live a more mindful and whole life.

Artress, Lauren, *Walking a Sacred Path*, New York: Riverhead Books, 1995.

Baldwin, Christina, *Life's Companion: Journal Writing as a Spiritual Quest*, New York: Bantam, 1990.

Bloom, William, *First Steps*, Scotland: Findhorn Press, 1993.

———, *Money, Heart, and Mind: Financial Well-being for People and Planet*, London: Viking, 1995.

Chopra, Deepak, *Unconditional Life*, New York: Bantam, 1991.

Csikszentmihalyi, Mihaly, *Flow: The Psychology of Optimal Experience*, New York: Harper & Row, 1990.

———, *The Evolving Self: A Psychology for the Third Millennium*, New York: HarperCollins, 1993.

Ferguson, Duncan S., ed., *New Age Spirituality*, Kentucky: Westminster/John Knox Press, 1993.

Leonard, George, *Mastery*, New York: Dutton, 1991.

Luks, Allan, and Pane, Peggy, *The Healing Power of Doing Good*, New York: Fawcett Columbine, 1991.

Marks, Linda, *Living with Vision*, Indianapolis: Knowledge Systems, 1989.

Matthews, Caitlin, *Singing the Soul Back Home*, Rockport, MA: Element, 1995.

Pennington, M. Basil, *Centering Prayer*, New York: Doubleday, 1980.

Simon, Sidney B., and Simon, Suzanne, *Forgiveness*, New York: Warner Books, 1991.

Sinetar, Marsha, *Developing a 21st-Century Mind*, New York: Villard Books, 1991.

———, *Do What You Love, The Money Will Follow*, New York: Paulist Press, 1987.

———, *Elegant Choices, Healing Choices*, New York: Paulist Press, 1988.

———, *Ordinary People as Monks and Mystics*, New York: Paulist Press, 1986.

———, *To Build the Life You Want, Create the Work You Love*, New York: St. Martin's Press, 1995.

Wakefield, Don, *Expect a Miracle*, San Francisco: HarperCollins, 1995.

DOING IT. These are books that deal with some aspect of manifestation, usually focusing upon a particular skill like raising energy through ritual or visualization or focusing.

Beck, Renee, and Metrick, Sydney Barbara, *The Art of Ritual*, Berkeley: Celestial Arts, 1990.

Bloom, William, *Sacred Times: A New Approach to Festivals*, Scotland: Findhorn Press, 1990.

———, *Meditation in a Changing World*, Glastonbury, England: Gothic Image, 1993.

Cameron, Julia, *The Artist's Way: A Spiritual Path to Higher Creativity*, New York: Tarcher, 1992.

Campbell, Peter A., and McMahon, Edwin M., *Bio-Spirituality: Focusing as a Way to Grow*, Chicago: Loyola University Press, 1985.

Gawain, Shakti, *Creative Visualization*, New York: Bantam, 1982.

Gendlin, Eugene, *Focusing*, New York: Bantam, 1981.

Glouberman, Dina, *Life Choices and Life Changes Through Imagework*, London (Boston): Mandala Books (Unwin Paperbacks), 1991.

Kabat-Zinn, Jon, *Full Catastrophe Living*, New York: Delacorte, 1990.

Langer, Ellen, *Mindfulness*, New York: Addison-Wesley, 1989.

Markham, Ursula, *Visualisation*, Shaftesbury, England: Element Books, 1989.

Sher, Barbara, *Wishcraft: How to Get What You Really Want*, New York: Ballantine, 1979.

———, *I Could Do Anything, If I Only Knew What It Was*, New York: Delacorte, 1994.

Sher, Barbara, and Gottlieb, Annie, *Teamworks!*, New York: Warner Books, 1989.

Steindl-Rast, David, *Gratefulness: The Heart of Prayer*, New York: Paulist Press, 1984.

Zdenek, Marilee, *Inventing the Future: Advances in Imagery That Can Change Your Life*, New York: McGraw-Hill, 1987.

About the Author

David Spangler is a writer and educator who describes himself as a "free-lance mystic." From 1965 to 1979, he taught classes in California and lectured throughout the United States on mysticism, creating a spiritual practice, and personal and cultural transformation. From 1970 to 1973, he served as a co-director and spokesperson for the Findhorn Foundation community in northern Scotland and continues a relationship as a friend and advisor to that community. During the late seventies and early eighties, David designed and taught classes in future studies, community development, and emerging new paradigms for the University of Wisconsin in Milwaukee. He has also taught classes in manifestation and spirituality on-line over the computer. He is a Lindisfarne Fellow and the President of the Lorian Association.

David's books include *Revelation: The Birth of a New Age*; *Emergence: The Rebirth of the Sacred*; and *Reimagination of the World*, co-authored with cultural historian William Irwin Thompson. In 1996, Findhorn Press will publish his *A Pilgrim in Aquarius: Spirituality and the New Age*.

David lives near Seattle, Washington, with his wife, Julie, two sons, two daughters, and a ferret named Pixie.

For information about on-line classes and discussions on manifestation or spirituality, or to share your manifestation stories, please contact the Lorian Association at its World Wide Web page at http://www.speakeasy.org/~lorian/, or for e-mail, contact lorianassn@aol.com.